The Jewish Publication Society of America
Philadelphia ☆ *5727/1967*

Zalman Shazar

Morning
Stars

☆

Translated from the Hebrew original,
KOCHVEI BOKER *(Tel Aviv:*
Am Oved Publishers, 1950; Seventh edition, 1966)
by Sulamith Schwartz Nardi.

Contents

☆
　☆
　　☆
☆
　☆

*Ever since the bitter tidings reached me that the
little town of my youth had been erased from
the earth, vivid memories of it, long hidden
away, have risen to fill my mind, and I who had
almost ceased to think of my town, found
myself preoccupied with it in every moment of
comparative quiet or enforced rest.*

Whenever, in the midst of the mighty and hopeful process of the ingathering of my people's survivors, winds of contention or misunderstanding began to blow, the people of my town would come to my mind as I had glimpsed them in my youth with all their lovable qualities and all their disturbing capriciousness. And the memories served as warning and consolation and guidance.

There was a parallel here to the way,
in my childhood, I had imagined our Father
Abraham—as the legend tells us—leaning
over the side of a narrow bridge that spanned
the River of Egypt. Astonishment and joy
overwhelmed him as, for the very first time,
he saw, mirrored in the water, the unveiled face
of Sarai his wife, with whom he had lived and
for whom he had labored so long, and whose
beauty he saw only now as he led her across the
waves to the dangers of the royal court.

And I as a little boy used to slip into the synagogue courtyard at twilight to look into the deep, narrow well in its center, and find all the way down in the water the brilliant stars that floated so exquisitely in the skies above.

Let

   us

      remember

         those

                  stars

               as

            they

         were

            in

               the

                  morning

                        of

                              life,

                           for

                           they

                     are

                  growing

               pale

                  and

                     the

                        well

                           itself

                           is

                     no

                  more.

Steibtz,
My Town

☆

I spent eleven years of my life—no more—in Steibtz. I was three when my parents brought me there, after a great fire swept through Mir, the nearby town that was my birthplace. And only a year after my bar mitzvah, Steibtz had become too limited for me and I began my wanderings to distant centers of learning. But those eleven years were the dawn of my youth, and the time of my *heder* studies. What I absorbed then was sealed in my spirit by the fire of love, and the inspiration of those first days has been with me ever since.

I have gone far from Steibtz and known many a town and city more important, wealthier, graced with more learning, more knowledge, and more of the wonders of the world. Yet this town of Steibtz is uniquely mine: nothing can take its place.

It was a simple little town, quite ordinary, not set apart by its learning, or charity, or educational institutions. On the contrary, it was Mir, not Steibtz, that boasted a famous yeshiva; it was in neighboring Koidenhove, and not in Steibtz, that a hasidic rabbi lived. I doubt very much whether at the time a single resident of Steibtz was famous outside the town limits. Its rich men were only of middling wealth, and it had very few truly erudite Jews.

I remember clearly that there were only four men in Steibtz who were called "Reb" both to their faces and when they were not present.

One of these was the saintly Reb Elinka, a wizened little man who looked like the dried fig of talmudic legend. I saw him every morning walking slowly from his low house up on Yurzdike to the Old Synagogue. As he passed by wrapped in his bald, old fur coat, with a woolen scarf around his neck, I knew that I was looking at holiness itself in all its gracious modesty.

There was Reb Yehoshua, the Gemorra teacher and *dayan*, religious judge, of the town. A bony, black-bearded, angry-eyed man, he ruled his pupils, grown boys though they were, with strap and cane.

Their reward, it was said, was that all of them knew how to solve every problem in *Tosphot*. And there was Reb Ahre, pious beyond reproach, who taught artisans *Hayei Adam* in the synagogue; desperately poor himself, he was always collecting money to give to the needy. As for Reb Abraham, the husband of Dabrulia the pitchmaker, he had been blind from his youth and studied the Torah fervently all his life. The synagogue was his home, the town his source of support.

These were the four who were called "Reb" by everyone and always. They lived in different parts of the town. All of them wore plush hats even on weekdays, and even though they were poverty stricken and completely undemanding, they were the pride of the town and in the eyes of its simple workers rare and wonderful beings, virtually supermen.

No, Steibtz in those days was not a center of learning, but it was without doubt a center of work— a town of laborers, strong-armed and muscular men. Though Koidenhove had its hasidic rabbi, it had no river. Though Mir had its renowned yeshiva, it had no railroad. Steibtz had both. It lay on the banks of the River Nieman, which rose at nearby Pesuchna and was covered with rafts floating all the way to mighty Koenigsberg. And a railway line passed through Steibtz on the way from Brisk in Lithuania to Moscow. The noisy, bustling river bank in Steibtz was one of its unique features, too. The entire stretch, from the iron bridge to the ferry over the river, was shaded by trees and covered with parts of boats under construction, rafts ready to be launched, piles of lumber of all sizes and types, heaps of withes used like ropes to bind the rafts. From dawn till the stars came out workers toiled and sweated here. Often after reading conventional discussions of Jewish "parasitism" in the Diaspora, I have found myself wanting to beg the pardon of these long-gone workers of Steibtz whom I knew in my youth. I remember them patching holes in the sides of boats with rope and fiber; lying on their backs on the ground under larger boats, with huge wooden hammers and long iron files in their hands, closing up cracks from the morning to late hours of the night; hammering away and singing while the breezes blew from the turbulent river. Not all of them were young. There were white-bearded ones, too, with large families, fathers with children and sometimes grandchildren.

How horrified the whole town was that ghastly night when the scaffolding snapped and a boat fell on the workers, and Berel Chashe-Breinas was pulled out from underneath crushed to death, still holding a hammer in his hand! And that accusation of parasitism—fruit of the earnest desire to reform the Jewish economic structure—how totally undeserved it was in your case, carpenters and boat builders of Steibtz; planers of boards and fasteners of rafts; carters that worked along with your horses to drag logs from the woods and throw them into the Nieman; transporters of barrels of tar to the boats; loaders and unloaders, tossed by rain and storm and wind during the long, long hours of your working day!

Our neighbors in their towns without river or forest ridiculed your earthy quality, your sturdiness and health. They themselves were pale and skinny, with shrunken stomachs: yeshiva students, housebound, almost never exposed to light and air. Amazed at your appetite when you sat down to table at the end of a back-breaking day in sun and rain and wind, they called you *Steibtzer Kishkes* ("Guts"). It was the custom to give each town a nickname, and this one accurately expressed the attitude toward Steibtz. But it was the carters and butchers of Steibtz, feared as they were by the peasants in the vicinity, who saved our town from attack and rushed to the defense of the Jews in towns close by.

Yet these simple, unlearned people of Steibtz had the most profound reverence for learning and respect for the learned.

Though the yeshiva was in Mir, crumbs from its table nourished all the towns of the area. So the *Batei Midrash*, the houses of learning of Steibtz received many a young man on his way to or out of the yeshiva—some who had come from such a distance that they were too late for the opening of the term; others who had turned skeptic and been forced to leave the yeshiva; students soon to be ordained who wished to study by themselves for a year without interruption; youthful kabbalists in search of uncensored solitude. The artisans of the town took it upon themselves to find lodgings for the young men and "days" for them to eat regularly in various houses. There was no *Bet Midrash* in the town without students in it, and no synagogue where the sound of learning was not heard all day and even till the small hours of the night.

The Old and New Synagogues were the special province of the younger students, but the *prushim*, who had left their families in some far-off town, found their place in the hasidic *shtiebel*. Needing to send money home for the support of their wives, the *prushim* could not simply make do with the meals given them in private homes; they did some teaching besides—instruction in Gemorra to some respectable householder or some brilliant youngster who had no more to learn in the *heder* and had not yet reached the yeshiva but was studying by himself in a synagogue. The *parush* would stand behind him and guide him along the uncharted paths of the Talmud. Between afternoon and evening prayers you found a *parush* teaching a whole group of townsmen at the wooden table behind the stove in the *Bet Midrash*— one taught *Hayei Adam* in the Talmud Torah building, another *Ein Yaakov* in the *shtiebel*.

There was much studying in Steibtz. In the Old

Synagogue a Gemorra lesson was led by the rabbi's young son-in-law, in the New Synagogue by Shlomo the *shochet*. In the artisans' *Bet Midrash* on Yurzdike, Iche Tanhums delighted his hearers by expounding chapters of the Bible in a sweetly sung melody and with the aid of sage and charming parables—to be sure, only on nights when Iche Tanhums was not engaged in reading from the Book of Job in the homes of mourners.

Aside from the yeshiva students and the *prushim*, for whom every hour of the day and night was a time for learning, not a few simple householders and artisans also set aside hours for study in the *Bet Midrash*. They would remain there after morning or evening prayers, entrenched at their *stenders*, each totally immersed in his book despite the bustling street outside and the worries of the market place and the river bank.

In the middle of the day Reb Shmuel Yehoshua, the shopkeeper, would come into the larger *Bet Midrash*. Though his shop was always full of customers, he could rely on his wife to manage the business. Opening a large Gemorra on the table behind the stove, he would try to recollect what he had learnt in Volozhin before his marriage.

And here was the blind Reb Abraham putting his soiled handkerchief on the open Gemorra he was studying from memory; he would beg one or another of the young men in the room to do him

the kindness of looking up the commentary in
Ktzot ha-Hoshen dealing with the page he had
reached.

Then the tall Yoshe Frades would walk in. Shopkeeper though he was, he opened his volume of the
Mishna and studied for a good full hour, reading in
a loud voice. He simply disregarded the unkind
comments to the effect that he was "working towards
a eulogy." Let the critics rail—he would go on
"studying like a bell," as they said in the town.

I was a child of the *shtiebel*, and though the
shtiebel was very near the Great Synagogue, my
relationship to the latter was quite distant. I occasionally went there with Father on Saturday afternoons before dark to hear some famous preacher who
had come from far away. Even more rarely I went
with Father to listen to the close of a service sung
by some famous cantor whose coming had been announced in notices on the walls of the *shtiebel*. On
such occasions, before the repetition of the *Amidah*,
a little group of lovers of cantorial music would leave
the *shtiebel* with their prayer shawls still on and
make their way into the packed synagogue to hear
the visiting cantor sing the Sanctification. There was
still another reason for going to the synagogue: to
hear a heart-breaking address in memory of a great
man who had just died. As I look back now, I see
that those memorial meetings served to link the

otherwise isolated town with the rest of the grieving Jewish people.

The distance between us and the Great Synagogue was thus sometimes bridged by a festive prayer, at other times by an impressive sermon, a crucial dispute or a public assembly on the choice of a rabbi or other communal matters. The large and perpetually unfinished New Synagogue seemed even more distant. It was no less *Mitnaged* in nature than the older synagogue, but there was far less learning in it: the town rabbi did not pray in it, and the respected householders entered it most infrequently. There was an air of controversy about it as there always is about a new institution. The town's established citizens were to be found among the leadership of the Old Synagogue or in the *shtiebel*, while the recipients of funds sent by relatives in America or South Africa gathered in the New Synagogue. If we of the *shtiebel* entered the New Synagogue, it was to enjoy the trills of its new cantor at the end of the Sabbath service or to listen to a Zionist speaker ardently holding forth before a listening crowd on Sabbath eve.

The *shtiebel* was a completely different matter. It was my second home and all the worshippers in it seemed members of the family, whether they were *Hasidim* by birth and founders of the *shtiebel* or townsmen who had joined it later. Even as a small child I knew each one's gestures and foibles, troubles and ailments, and I wondered why my fellow-pupils in the *heder* did not sense the enormous distinction between worshippers in the *shtiebel* and outsiders. The members of the *shtiebel* were in fact constant visitors to our house. They came to Father for help when they were hard-pressed; Mother worried about them when they were ill. They drank tea with Father on Saturday nights; they danced with him till dawn on the night of Shemini Atzeret, the eighth day of Succot—they danced in the house and the *shtiebel,* the market place and the street. How different from each other and how close to each other they were, how torn by factionalism—and how dear all of them were to me!

Old Reb Elinka and Reb Yehoshua, the teacher, sat as *dayanim* with the town rabbi in complicated cases and particularly when a divorce was under consideration. It was to Steibtz that the neighboring communities, too, brought divorce cases. On a day when a divorce was to be taken up Reb Elinka was invariably depressed. Bitter sighs punctuated his slow walk from his little house at the edge of Yurzdike to the rabbi's house where the court sat. And the Gemorra students of Reb Yehoshua were free of their teacher's high-handed domination that day and could do their studying by themselves in whatever synagogue they wished. The blind Reb Abraham profited by it all—there were so many bright, unoccupied children about, who could look up references in commentaries for him and help him solve problems that came to his mind as he studied Talmud from memory.

The *shochtim*, ritual slaughterers, followed after the *dayanim* in religious significance. There were two: Reb Eliahu and Reb Shloime. Though for decades, both in the slaughter house outside the town and in their own courtyards, they had slaughtered cattle for the butchers and fowl for the housewives and heard the cows groaning and seen the chickens writhing at their feet and flashed their rigorously sharpened knives and stained their long coats with blood—for all that, strangely enough, the two of them were the kindest of men and so gentle that they seemed incapable of hurting a fly. There was a vague sense of hostility between the two households, but the underlying kindliness of both *shochtim* seemed to smooth over the difficulties, and an outsider would never have suspected that there was any tension. Reb Eliahu's sphere of influence was the Old Synagogue, Reb Shloime's the New, and there was no open break between them.

Reb Eliahu was the veteran *shochet* of the two, but he was much more than a *shochet*. The town wits used to say that he had so many occupations you could people a whole community with him. Besides being a slaughterer, he was the reader in the Old Synagogue, he blew the *shofar* on the High Holy

Days, he was the chief *mohel* performing circumcisions in the town, and he was renowned as a matchmaker, having good connections with the best matchmakers in the country and serving all the wealthy families of the vicinity. He took the place of a Government-appointed rabbi, keeping a register of births and arranging certificates. In addition to all this, he spent hours every day cutting gravestones and carving ornamental designs on them: hands lifted in blessing in the case of a member of the priestly class; pitchers of water for libation in the case of a Levite; chopped down trees to indicate young lives that had been prematurely ended. And he carved rhymed eulogies in verse of his own composition on the stones: the Hebrew was most elegant and the letters at the beginning of the lines gave you the names of the dead.

He had still another truly unique occupation—nowadays we would say he operated an employment agency for rabbis. His net was flung far; he knew when a rabbinical post in some distant town became vacant either because the rabbi departed this life or because the laymen could no longer abide him. In each case he knew exactly whom to recommend, whether it was some rabbi who felt that he could not remain in the post he had, or a strange and wonderful *parush* about to enter the rabbinate. They all came knocking at his door—young rabbis, fathers-in-law with learned young sons-in-law, communal-minded householders, both intriguers and lovers of peace. Reb Eliahu found time for them despite his dozen diverse occupations. The match between rabbi and town was predetermined in the heavens, he insisted, exactly like the match between young man and girl. Tradition tells us that forty days before the birth of a child its future mate is announced on high: the assignment of rabbi to town is also announced, but out of reverence for learning, Reb Eliahu explained, the statement is made discreetly and the actual mating of the two is therefore harder to effect than the splitting of the Red Sea.

Clearly, Reb Eliahu's sources of income were many; some hard, some easy, some conventional, some unconventional. But the end result of them all was that he had the greatest difficulty in providing for his wife, his sons and daughters and sons-in-law and their children. All his long life he was a poor man. But he was a very dignified and serene poor man, a wise and gentle one. I spent much time in his home during my childhood, for his youngest son, Mottel, was my friend and my fellow-student from the time we entered *heder* till he left to study in the yeshiva at Maletz. Never once did I see Reb Eliahu imposing his will on his family. He was always mild and full of smiles—when he slaughtered chickens, when he circumcised infants, when he put the town register into order, when he sang liturgical tunes, when he hammered at stones. Reb Eliahu straddling the monuments in his yard was no different from Reb Eliahu tranquilly drinking tea at our table after evening prayers, listening to the conversation around him and thoughtfully discussing matches between young couples and problems of far-off and nearby communities in whose affairs he mixed with the same quiet deliberation that he mixed the tea Mother served him.

His voice was sweet and controlled when he read the Torah in the synagogue and prayed before the congregation on holidays. He was no cantor, to be sure, and he had no musical training, but he was master of the traditional melodies and the chant seemed to sing tenderly in his throat—Mother used to say, "There's a violin there, in his throat." Though he was particularly devoted to the Great Synagogue, he felt as the *shochet* for the *whole* community that he must occasionally appear before the worshippers in the other synagogues.

In the *shtiebel* every Yom Kippur we looked forward to his coming and chanting the Musaf Service. When the reading from the Bible was finished in the Great Synagogue, he would put on his heavy coat over his robe and *tallit* (this was a precaution against catching a cold) and would slowly make his way in rubbers through the synagogue courtyard from the Old Synagogue to our *shtiebel*. Since we read fewer of the additional poetic pieces in the service, we were already waiting expectantly. A fresh new spirit entered with him. The tired congregants wrapped their prayer shawls more securely around themselves, sighed deeply, and prepared to listen to Reb Eliahu. And he in his white robe and light socks, his *tallit* drawn over his head, walked very slowly to the reader's lectern. Carefully he pulled a special shelf out of it to judge the distance at which he should stand, so that he would later be able to kneel without having to move from his place. His graying beard rose slightly out of the concealing folds of the *tallit*, and in imploring, anguished tones he sang the beginning of the Reader's Prayer: "O behold me, destitute of good works. . . . " Then he grew still, and while all of us held our breaths, he chanted on in a low voice until suddenly he burst forth into a powerful outcry: "And rebuke Satan that he may not accuse me!"

Entreaty began again in measured tones—and then low trilling, as if he were diving far down, sobbing as he struggled to rise, till at last he emerged triumphantly out of the depths and his voice was loud and clear as he trod the beaten path of the Reader's Repetition of the *Amidah*.

How stirred one small boy was by this heartfelt praying!

Then we reached the sequence of "the sins that we have sinned," and the whole congregation moved, each within his *tallit*, as the trees in a forest move when a storm passes over them. Reb Eliahu stirred, too, and then suddenly came to rest. During that momentary spell of calm between the storms, his warm voice sang out the entreaty, "And for all these, God of forgiveness, forgive us, pardon us, grant us atonement."

I could practically feel the taut, quivering strings of the violin in his throat, trembling with a spiritual vibration that plucked at our hearts. . . .

During those moments it seemed to me impossible that this was the same Reb Eliahu whom we saw sitting at our table in deep discussion with my uncle while he drank tea with Mother; the same Reb Eliahu who stood in our hallway the day before Yom Kippur, covering the blood stains on his arms after he slaughtered the chickens to serve as symbolic atonement; and—even more incredible—the same Reb Eliahu who scolded my friend Mottel for not wanting to go to *heder*. I would have said that the Reb Eliahu standing before us in the *shtiebel* was the biblical "man clothed in linen," pleading before our Father in Heaven, participating in the Heavenly Choir.

Actually, under his direction the whole congregation became a choir, singing together "And the Cohanim, ay, ay, ay. . . ." When they did this and when Father left his seat to stand at Reb Eliahu's right, with the rebbe at his left, both of them hurrying to rise from their kneeling posture to help Reb Eliahu get up in perfect perpendicular stance like

that of the ministering angels above—then I knew
that the comparison in my mind was neither forced
nor inappropriate. . . .

Very few in the town knew of the strained relationship between Reb Eliahu and the somewhat
younger *shochet*, Reb Shloime; in fact there were almost no visible signs of tension. It had something
to do, it seemed, with vested rights, and the percent-
age of the meat tax assigned to the slaughterer—
subtle points which could hardly arouse public concern. That the wives of the two slaughterers were
not on cordial terms, though they lived near each
other, was perceptible, but the men themselves
could be seen every weekday morning walking side
by side like a pair of twins, each with his prayer
shawl and phylacteries in a bag under his arm. They
parted only when they reached the synagogue courtyard. Here the tall, lean, absent-minded Reb Shloime
turned off to the New Synagogue, while Reb Eliahu,
the shorter, older and more practical of the two, went
on in his deliberate fashion to the Old Synagogue
where the prayers never began till he arrived.

Curiously, when the Zionist movement came to
Steibtz it supplied a legitimate, public reason for the
old, almost impalpable conflict. Though Reb Eliahu
did not actually become a Zionist, he never fought
against the new ideology. He knew and never ob-
jected to the fact that his oldest son, Ahre, not only
bought the shekel of membership in the Zionist

Organization, but sold many a shekel to others. Reb Eliahu's relations with matchmakers and rabbinical circles in the outside world had taught him that Zionism was now to be accepted as a fact of life. Reb Shloime, however, was one of the fanatical opponents, and with Shaul of the bathhouse and other faithful disciples of the town rabbi, seized every opportunity to weaken and destroy the movement.

In Reb Eliahu's family Zionist activity was not confined to Ahre, the eldest son who later succeeded his father as *shochet*, stone cutter and registrar. Reb Eliahu's youngest son, my friend Mottel Machtey, was to become a leader of the Labor Zionist group in the town. On the other hand, Reb Shloime's eldest son, Yehoshua, went to study in the Slabodka Yeshiva where he became famous for his scholarship. When during World War I the rabbi of Steibtz left the town, Reb Yehoshua came to serve in his place. The result was that after the old rabbi returned from Saratov, the town was torn between supporters of the old rabbi and supporters of Reb Yehoshua. The controversy went on bitterly for years, one party being led by Reb Shloime and his family, and the other by Reb Eliahu and his.

Till the Holocaust came and "made peace" between them.

Actually, Reb Eliahu and Reb Shloime had each died at a ripe old age before the great cataclysm, but the conflict between their children continued until the evil times. Both their eldest sons found their eternal rest in the common grave the Jews of Steibtz were forced to dig for themselves the day after Yom Kippur in 1942.

Ahre, son of Reb Eliahu, had a son who settled in the Land of Israel and became a member of the Jewish Police Force: a son of this son was later to fall in the struggle for the Land. Ahre himself visited the Land only half a year before World War II began. He accepted a post as *shochet* in one of the quarters of Tel Aviv and returned to Steibtz— briefly, he thought—to wind up his affairs and make sure that the community would accept his son-in-law as *shochet* in his stead. But he was never to see Tel Aviv again.

As for Reb Yehoshua, the son of Reb Shloime, his position as rabbi of the community was no longer contested after the old rabbi passed away; he even established a sort of yeshiva. And from the very few survivors of Steibtz I heard how when the end came he wrapped himself in his prayer shawl, put on his phylacteries, and solemnly recited *Vidu*—the death bed confession—with all the people of the town. Reciting the Psalms, he walked before them all to meet death.

Whooping
Cough

☆

When was it? At the beginning of the beginning, when I was about eight years old and still a pupil in the second *heder*, the one we called the Bible *heder*. It was about a year and a half after I left my first teacher, the *Dardeke Melamed*, who taught the youngest children to read. With the second teacher we studied Gemorra in the afternoons only; most of our time was spent on the Prophetic Books and the Writings. We had just finished learning the Book of Proverbs by heart and had plunged into the glorious depths of Isaiah, while in Gemorra

the winter term had been spent on "He who puts
down the pitcher" and the summer term on "He who
entrusts." It was winter again and we were at the
gates of *Baba Metzia*, concerned with "Two who
hold," and suddenly whooping cough got hold of
me and would not let go. All my mother's remedies
were to no avail, though she was so knowing and
experienced about children's diseases. My thin little
body was wracked by the cough and knew no rest.
Finally our warm-hearted, pleasant Dr. Levitan
prescribed a change of climate.

It seemed strange and practically unnatural to
interrupt my studies in the middle of the *heder*'s
busy term. And for my worried mother the thought
of sending a badly chilled child out into the raging
winter was almost unendurable. But since there was
such implicit trust in the doctor and no other cure
was known, Mother had to agree. My father was
preparing for one of his trips to the woods, and it
was decided that I should go with him.

We left at noon on a sunny day, with winter
flaming at its most intense. Father was wrapped in
a series of fur coats covered by a heavy, dark robe
with a red wool belt, and a red wool shawl at his
throat. Raising the high, yellow collar that concealed
both his face and the black caracul hat on his head,
and seeming to grow larger and wider, he completely filled half the front seat of the sleigh. As for

me, I was lost inside a heap of borrowed coats and robes, all too long and wide, that surrounded and bound and concealed me. Woolen boots encased my legs up to the knees and above, and a yellow, gold-edged shawl covered my face completely, except for my two eyes, which were wide open, absorbing all the whiteness of the new, blinding, shining world that sang a melody of strength I had never heard before.

From the town we made our way to a stretch of country where a few weeks earlier the River Nieman had overflowed its banks. The river was gone now and the sound of its waves was silenced. It was wrapped in a thick layer of mute ice and the ice itself was covered by a furry white coat of glittering snow—just like Father and me and the driver who sat in front, and the sleigh. For the whole world around us was covered with white light "as with a garment. . . ."

Here where the Nieman had flowed not long ago, that white garment, so calm, so levelling and so deceptive, had to be treated with particular prudence. For here, underneath their heavy robe, the waves still tossed. Here you must be careful, driver! The mighty forces in the depths might begin to rage and storm and tear the deceptive mask of calm to bits; then the ground that seemed so solid under the horse's hooves would become the battlefield of op-

posing powers that rose up against each other,
drowned each other and sucked down into the abyss
anything above them. Beware, O mortal man!

One had to be doubly careful here. Only a few
nights past this had been the scene of a mysterious
procession, with people bearing crosses and ikons.
The Orthodox priest had poured holy water, children had sung choral chants, and at midnight by the
light of lanterns and torches of burning pitch, peasants armed with hatchets and saws had hacked a
gigantic cross out of this quiet ice.

Time and again we *heder* children had been
warned that we must not show ourselves in the streets
during those religious processions. It was said that
the mere appearance of a Jewish child might unleash
the most dangerous passions in the masses of peasants already incited by a night of Christian fervor.
With bated breath we used to sit at home behind
closed shutters, looking through the cracks at the
priests in gorgeous robes, the splendid holy pictures,
the choir of bright-ribboned girls who filled the air
of our Jewish street and the street of the Old Synagogue with the chords of strange, monotonous, shrill
and terrifying songs. This long, hushed, disquieting
curfew lasted until there were no more voices outside and our Christian servant girl burst into the
house, crimson with frost and shining with joy,
eager to tell us how wonderful it had all been and
how the cross had been set up in glory and holiness.

Then we would breathe freely again and Father would open the shutters. . . .

And now in the woods that giant cross, sparkling with frost, stood near us and threatened our whole town.

Somewhere near it lurked the unseen pit, crisscrossed by axes, the holy pit out of which the cross had been cut on that fearful night. The pit was open to the lowering depths—how careful the coachman had to be here!

From the chained, voiceless river the sleigh slid directly to the wood of Zadvoriya. How different it was now from the green and pleasant place where we loved to stroll on summer evenings and where the weak and sickly of the town came to convalesce! The paths seemed changed, and you could not recognize the trees that had been green and full of birds. Now the birds were all gone and the trees looked like white-wrapped scarecrows, each with many arms. Or were they like corpses in eternal shrouds? The only cheerful thing was the strong light that poured down on all of them and shone out of all of them, while the song of the snow crackling under the horse's hooves and the sleigh's tracks seemed a festive announcement of the everlasting spring within the frozen whiteness.

As we went on, my breath became rising mist and Father's mustache stiffened when he spoke, but the white radiance shed joy on everything around

☆

us. Inside of me, under all the coats and all the fur, like the waves stirring beneath their icy cover, my heart was gay and full of song because of the spring-like flame of that gleaming winter, so strong and so shining, pouring life so abundantly upon the world. We were headed towards Anufrova, a forest-estate between the two little towns of Mohilna and Uzda. The wood here was being cut by a wealthy Jewish merchant from Vilna; Father was his agent and to some extent his partner. The pines grew densely in Anufrova, and it took many hours to walk through them. German appraisers in short fur coats strode along, calculating precisely how many boards, railroad ties, thresholds, or posts each tree would make. Jewish clerks wrote down their estimates, and then father computed costs and prices. Reb Shlomo the "marker," wrapped in his hairy sheepskin coat, strode along the whole winter day, going from one cut tree trunk to another with a hammer in his hand. The initials of the owners of the forest were on the hammer, and Reb Shlomo brought it down forcefully on the chopped wood so as to impress the initials on the top. How eager I was to take the hammer from him and "print" those letters myself, and how bitterly disappointed I was when I discovered that even though I struck out with all my strength, not a single letter was stamped on the wood. I learned then that enormous strength was needed if letters were to be engraved properly. And from Vassily the stableman I learned many other mysteries and delights of the woods.

People worked in Anufrova all day but never slept there. During part of the week they spent the nights in an inn at Mohilna, and the rest of the week in an inn in Uzda on the other side of the forest. They went home for Saturday.

This was the way the forest workers lived during the woodcutting season, and we did the same.

Even by the standards of our tiny towns, Mohilna was pitifully small. Its one strong point was its nearness to Pesuchna, the place at which the River Nieman started its course and near which there lived an extraordinary Polish nobleman named Yutka, famous throughout the neighborhood for his very great wealth and his equally great eccentricity. At Pesuchna the Nieman was still very narrow, and the timber merchants had to go to Mohilna to start floating their wide rafts down the stream. They had no choice but to stay at the inn in Mohilna, and the inn was of course the center of the little town's life.

When we arrived at the inn, the Hebrew teacher I found there told me that the innkeeper had very distinguished connections which raised the prestige of the whole town. The innkeeper's name was, as we knew it, Reb Shemuel Mohilner; the German appraisers called him "Herr Goldberg." He was, the teacher said, brother to the Hebrew storywriter who lived in Minsk and was known by the pen name of Yacnehaz—the initials of Yeshaya Cohen Nissan Har-Zahav (the last name being the Hebrew translation of Goldberg). How new and exciting I found it all! The Hebrew writer had so cleverly turned the ordinary name of Goldberg into the rare Hebrew Har-Zahav, and Yaknehaz, the abbreviation so well known to everybody from the Prayer Book,* into the pen name of Yacnehaz. And here right before my eyes was a real live brother of a famous Hebrew writer, and that brother waited upon the timber merchants and agents who worked with us in Anufroval

We stayed in Uzda for just one day. It was larger than Mohilna and the inn was something like a real hotel. I still remember the tall house with the veranda running around it, on a corner of the long, sloping street. I remember equally well how impressed I was by the plentiful food prepared for the timber merchants. I had seen nothing like it at the inn in Mohilna or even in homes in our town. It reminded me of the feast the bearers of the Burial Society—the Hevra Kadisha—used to have at their annual celebration on the fifteenth of Kislev. Even the fleshy face of the innkeeper, who supervised all that cramming, has remained in my memory. It was the face of an energetic man, intent on becoming

* Yaknehaz consists of the first letters of the Hebrew words: Yain, Kiddush, Ner, Havdala, Zeman: the order of the blessings in the Kiddush on a festival falling on Saturday night.

rich, serving his guests with every bit of his being; he tried hard to win my childish heart, but he failed.

Years later I learned that Uzda had entered Hebrew literature under the name of Zuzukovke, the town whose houses and streets, saints and villains live in the pages of Devora Baron's stories. I liked to imagine her heroes and heroines in the setting of the long, sloping street I remembered having seen from the veranda of the inn during the "whooping-cough journey" of my childhood.

At the end of the week, while the sleigh was taking us home, something dreadful happened. Until we reached Svirzna, the town right before ours, we had travelled in the gayest of moods, reflecting the joy that sparkled out of the festive winter. At Svirzna we met travellers returning from our own Steibtz. Their faces were dark with grief. The night before, we found out, a coachman had taken this same road with a sleigh full of passengers from a number of towns. He had lost his way, and near the tall cross on the ice the sleigh had plunged down into the holy pit that the axes had criss-crossed and laid open. The fire brigade came and pulled most of the passengers out of the water; they were now in the hospital. But the driver and one man from Svirzna had drowned in the stormy depths, and the firemen drew up their lifeless bodies. The whole of Svirzna went to the funeral and, in fact, the travellers who told us the story were themselves returning from the funeral. Before we parted, they warned us again and again to be careful, for it was the end of the month and the nights were dark despite all the snow, and that pit was still open. . . .

The bad news left us stunned. The driver, a good friend of the one who had drowned, sighed bitterly and whipped the horse on.

When the road was normal, it took twenty minutes from Svirzna to Steibtz. We travelled for half an hour, for three-quarters of an hour, and there was still not even a glimpse of the fords near the town or of the tall church on the hill inside of it. The driver got out of the sleigh, groped around in the dark, and returned to inform us that we were lost.

I have no notion how long we went on circling between the bushes on the bank and the snow on the river, with absolutely no sense of road or direction. It seemed forever. The wet, pricking snow, robbed of its splendor by darkness and grief, beat down mercilessly and obliterated every sign of a path. Our experienced driver was completely bewildered. Where had the famous wood disappeared to? Where was the iron bridge over which the trains crossed the river? Why was the church spire not to be seen? The snow covered all the familiar landmarks and the darkness annihilated all dividing lines. The sad news had unsettled us all. The driver kept lashing the horse, the snow lashed at our faces, and the little boy, his heart full of sadness and concern, was crushed by the inevitability of the danger lurking somewhere near in the whirling night in that holy, criss-crossed pit leading directly down to the abyss which had just swallowed its victims—the pit whose hidden mouth was waiting wide-open for us. And then sudenly a whistle and a flash of light came from the evening train which flew by along the tracks close to us!

"*Tfu!*" the sweating driver spat. "The devil with it, we're in back of Zadvoriya!"

He turned the sleigh back at once, whipped the horse with all his might, and within half an hour brought us on to the dear, familiar street of our town, straight to the veranda of our house, where Mother stood waiting with impatience and longing.

Her hands shook as she took the belt off my robe and the robe off my fur coat and the fur coat off my cloth coat and the cloth coat off my suit, and then gently felt my forehead—and found it flaming hot while all my body was covered with a cold sweat.

She undressed me and put me to bed and gave me hot tea with raspberry jam to drink, while my sister was sent to bring Dr. Levitan at once.

Shabbatai Zevi
in My Childhood

As soon as I began to study the mystery of Shabbatai Zevi and the movement he inspired, I found myself trying to remember how I had happened to know his name even before I read anything about him. In what circumstances and in what tone had it first been mentioned in my hearing? For a long time I could not find the answer. The mass of information I had accumulated from books was so great that the first layer of childhood impressions seemed completely covered over.

Suddenly, during a quiet moment, my first encounter with his name rose to the surface of my memory exactly as it had taken place so many years earlier. It was connected with old Mendel Lifschitz, a wealthy, pious and highly respected man in our town. He was not really a native but had struck root among us many years back, owning a large house near the market, inside the courtyard of one of the wealthy townsmen. Most of Mendel Lifschitz' life had been spent in the large cities of Russia or in Koenigsberg over the border, and it was only recently that he had returned to live comfortably and quietly among us. He was no longer active in business, and his children were all married and scattered over the world. When his wife died, Mendel Lifschitz did something the town found most unusual. He began to build a free school for poor children as a memorial to her. This Talmud Torah was to stand in the synagogue court, and the construction of the large building went on for years. From time to time the red brick walls grew visibly higher and then stopped at some particular point. Occasionally the old man and a clean-shaven stranger were seen walking on the scaffolding, measuring and calculating and measuring again. People said that the building had "eaten" close to two thousand rubles and was sure to "eat" a thousand more before it was finished. This figure of speech baffled me completely. How could a building eat money? There was something else even more unclear to me: it was reported that

Mendel Lifschitz intended to have handicrafts taught in the school, as well as Hebrew studies. Do you need books to train a boy to be a smith? And what connection could there possibly be between Abraham the teacher and technical things?

Though far from fanaticism, Reb Mendel was scrupulously observant of religious precept and custom. Neat in his ways, careful in his speech, generous and charitable, he took no part in disputes and wished for neither position nor honor. He was one of the faithful supporters of our town rabbi. And the rabbi was a fearful, militant anti-Zionist. When a Hebrew library was founded by our first Zionists, the enraged rabbi sent a bill of excommunication to the owner of the house where the library had been opened. By the next morning the bookcases were all out in the street. Another time when the Zionists arranged a Hanukkah celebration, the rabbi had the *shamash* announce that by order of the rabbi and officers of the synagogue attendance at the celebration was absolutely forbidden. It was from the rabbi's sermon one Sabbath of Repentance that I first learnt of the existence of the Zionist thinker, Ahad Ha-Am. The rabbi wrathfully waved a red handkerchief in his clenched hand and shouted: "Ahad Ha-Am and Lilienblum, for them an evil doom!" The rhyme impressed itself on my childish mind and left the names deeply engraved upon my memory.

Loyal to the rabbi, Mendel Lifschitz, too, was

among the opponents of Zionism which had just made its way into our town and captured most of the liberal members of our family. Despite my father's inclination toward Zionism and his critical attitude toward the rabbi, Father, who was a *Hasid* and in his early forties, and Mendel, who was a *Mitnaged* of seventy, enjoyed each other's company and on summer evenings went for walks together outside the town limits. And I went with them.

I must confess that I was not too enthusiastic about those joint walks. There were too many long pauses for my taste. Mendel Lifschitz walked with measured steps and whenever he wanted to stress a point or to listen very carefully to something Father was saying, he came to a stop right there on the path. Short, broad-bearded, with his thumb stuck in his belt, he stood still, concentrating on the matter under discussion. As for me, I liked to walk fast, and when we left the town behind us and followed the railroad tracks, my greatest pleasure was to jump along the wooden ties between the tracks without ever touching the ground. Since Father insisted on my keeping within his sight, I had to interrupt my progress and jump back when they stood still.

Though the pauses annoyed me, I found the conversations between the pauses fascinating. One day Father, whose attachment to Zionism was then beginning, tried to explain to the antagonistic Mendel that the sublime and the ridiculous were curiously mingled in the movement. The sublimity lay in the very nature of the idea, and what was amusing was the resemblance between the cliquishness of Zionists as he saw it now and the cliquishness of Hasidism as he had known it in his youth. Most amusing of all was the fact that the enlightened Zionists were totally unaware of the resemblance, and did not even begin to suspect its existence.

"Reb Mendel, believe me, when Michael Shemi Horowitz came back from the Congress in Basel and began to talk about Dr. Herzl, I felt as if I were listening to our Habad preacher in Dubrovna, talking about the rebbe on his return from Lubavitch after the High Holy Days."

"And I tell you, Reb Leib"—Mendel stopped walking, lifted his hand and shook his finger in grave warning—"I tell you that a thing like this movement of yours can only be judged by its results. It is a very serious matter. God forgive me, but the end of Dr. Herzl may easily be like Shabbatai Zevi's."

Father turned pale and shuddered. He who so disliked arguments and disputes recoiled and raised his hands defensively. "What is this you're saying, Reb Mendel? What is this you're saying? Do you hear your own words?"

"Reb Leib, this is what I'm afraid of. *Eretz*

Yisrael was not regained then, and it will not be regained now. And the end will be the same bitter end."

Father was so hurt and grieved that he could not go on with the discussion. He turned back and they finished their walk.

I can still see Mendel Lifschitz' warning finger and Father's pallor and sudden reversal of direction.

At the end of the walk when we were within the town, Mendel tried to placate Father and at the same time to make his own objections clearer. He resorted to a kind of parable.

"Reb Leib, you know our physician, Dr. Levitan? Could anyone doubt his devotion to his patients? Once there was a sick child at whose bedside he sat night after night, bringing him medicines, paying for what he needed—practically sacrificing himself for the child's sake. The child recovered and the town rang with stories about the doctor's efforts and dedication. Now imagine that the opposite happened and the child died despite everything the doctor did. Do you think that in that case any one would praise the doctor's devotion and all the trouble he went to? That's what I meant, Reb Leib, when I said that one judges these things by how they end. And I am afraid of what the end may be, terribly afraid, Reb Leib. . . ."

Father's
Library

☆

How far back can I trace my love of books and libraries? To the time, I believe, when at the age of eight or nine I was first permitted on the eve of Passover to help Father air his books and dust them to make sure that they were absolutely free of leaven.

When I read Hermann Hesse's lovely essay on his grandfather's library, the first he had seen in his childhood, and the source of his feeling for books, I was reminded irresistibly of my father's book shelves. Where are they now and where are all the houses that had such libraries?

My father was neither writer nor rabbi but simply a merchant, for the most part a rather busy merchant. His library was not by any means one of the largest in the town. The rabbi's library contained many more volumes; the library of the *dayan* had more books on Jewish law, and the son-in-law of our wealthiest man had a more extensive collection of Hebrew literature. Father's was an average collection, the library of a moderately learned householder. However, he never chose his books haphazardly or for the mere purpose of decoration; each in its own way was vitally necessary for him at some particular time.

Why was it that I was chosen to assist in airing the books? I had sisters who were older than I but on whom Father clearly felt he could not rely. The main point was knowing how to put the books back in their proper place and order. How could the girls possibly know that?

They were, to be sure, involved in the process of taking the books out of the cases into the yard where long boards had been placed on the backs of benches and chairs. On those boards the books, large and small, were laid one by one, all of them open for the wind to leaf through, like some keen-minded scholar glancing through them repeatedly in the course of several hours. In the meantime

Mother went over all of them with a goose feather, cleaning the sides and backs carefully so as to remove any suspicion of leaven. When dusk came it was time to take the books off the boards and return them to the shelves. And then it was only to me that Father could look for help.

To this day I remember how the books were arranged. I was not yet acquainted with their contents, but I learned Father's system from him and made sure not to forget it. He had no written catalog, of course, but in "the nature of things" every book had its appointed place. It was self-understood that the *Tanya*, small and thin as it was, should stand alongside the large *Torah-Or*, so well bound in black cloth, and in the vicinity of the *Likutei Torah*, which resembled the *Torah-Or* in size and binding, and of the *Zemach Zedek*, the *Noam Elimelech*, the *Kidushat ha-Levi*, the *Ohev Yisrael*—all of them the work of the fathers of Hasidism. Even though I already knew that *Der Alter Rebbe** who had written the *Tanya* was the same as the author of the *Shulhan Arukh* of the Rav, I understood that the two were not to be placed near each other but that this *Shulhan Arukh* must be on the second shelf near the *Yoreh Dea* and *Hayei Adam* and the various editions of *Hoshen Mishpat* and *Even ha-Ezer*.

---

* *Der Alter Rebbe* (the Old Rabbi) is the affectionate name in Habad for Reb Schneur Zalman, the founder of that hasidic sect.

Then there was the Old Rabbi's large Siddur, two square volumes full of wine stains on the pages that contained the Passover Haggadah, and spotted with tears where the Rosh Hashanah *Amidah* prayer appeared. This Siddur was not to be set near other ordinary prayer books that were used every day. It was in fact the book with which the library opened, the book that stood at the head of the first shelf. Next to it was the large Haggadah with many commentaries that Father followed in conducting our own *seder*. Alongside of the Haggadah was the *Kitzur Sheloh*, though it was smaller than the Siddur and Haggadah. This seventeenth-century classic of Ashkenazi mysticism was the book that my grandfather used to ask me to climb up and take down for him whenever he visited us, so that he might carry it to morning prayers in the *shtiebel*. He would put it in his *tallit* bag along with the *Hok le-Yisrael* which he always brought with him from home.

Near the *Kitzur Sheloh* there was a thin volume the sight of which invariably filled me with awe. This was the marvellous *Book of the Angel Raziel* which, everybody knew, was guaranteed to save households from fire. The fact that fires broke out frequently in our town did not weaken our faith in the book's magical qualities. (In a jesting mood Mother sometimes said: "You see the book itself wasn't burnt! That's proof!") When the *Angel Raziel* was opened to the wind in our yard, the wonderful pictures

seemed to step out of its pages and the whole yard
took on something of their miraculous nature.

Father's library did not include the complete
Talmud. The *shtiebel* owned the large edition published by Rom in Vilna. Those were black, cloth-
bound books stamped on the back with golden
letters, and Father always took whatever Gemorra
he was studying from the set in the *shtiebel*. I remember the day when that Talmud was first brought
to the *shtiebel*. The celebration was just like that
when a new Scroll of the Law is placed in the Ark.
Honey cake and brandy were served, and each of
the worshippers was given the privilege of carrying
a volume of the Talmud as if it were a banner. We
heder children were permitted to join the procession
—and even to take a few steps with a Gemorra in
hand. I remember how my heart beat when I lifted
the precious heavy tractate and bore it through the
synagogue courtyard!

There were, to be sure, many single volumes
of the Talmud in Father's library—left-overs of complete sets and tractates that were studied in *heder*.
There was an old edition of *Gittin* that I recall very
clearly—on the fast day of Tisha b'Av we used it to
study "Amar Rabbi Yohanan" on the Destruction. I
can recall various editions of the tractate *Shabbat*
and one of *Nedarim* with the commentary of Ha-
Ran. They stood next to the Mishna, the books arranged in proper order and clearly stamped with

numbers. Nearby were volumes of legends and parables—*Ein Yaakov, Midrash Rabba, Midrash Tan-
huma, Tanna de-Bei Eliyahu, Yalkut Shimoni,* all of
them very well-thumbed for they were read every
Saturday. Somewhat less worn were the Zohar and
a few homiletic books—*Yaarot Devash, Klei Yakar,
Arvei Nachal.* Below them were the *Mikraot Gedo-
lot,* published by Rom—the Five Books of Moses
with thirty-two commentaries: impressive-looking
volumes which were purposely set on a shelf
low enough for us children to reach. And we enjoyed them immensely, deriving special pleasure
from the legendary description of King Solomon's
wonderful throne which could be found in only one
place, the Aramaic *Targum Sheni* that appeared in
the *Mikraot.* There were other Bibles on that shelf:
one with Mendelsohn's commentary; newly printed
ones with Ibn Ezra's commentary and *Metzudat Zion*
and *Metzudat David*; an old one with heavy bluish
pages; a Jewish-German commentary; and, of course,
the tiny complete Bible that was a present from
Grandfather.

When Father got up on Saturday mornings, the
entire household was still asleep with the exception
of myself who only pretended to be. He would put
on his robe, say the *Shema* by himself, so that he
might come late to the *shtiebel,* and take out of the
bookcase a large beautifully printed Gemorra, the
one then being studied in the *shtiebel* by the Hevra

Shas. After preparing the section for the day, he would go to the *shtiebel*. In the afternoon, when he got up from his nap, he would draw me close to him and we would go over a chapter of *Torah-Or* or *Likutei Torah* together. These were taken down from the top shelf, while sometimes what we studied was from a Midrash on the second shelf. On winter Saturdays we would occasionally read the *Hafetz Hayim,* which despite its mitnagdic origin, was placed near the hasidic books.

Of the reference books, I remember particularly well the *Arukh ha-Shalem* and the *Mishpat ha-Urim*; Alexander Kohut's *Milin de Rabanan,* which listed sayings of the Sages in alphabetical order; *Zecher Rav,* where the roots of all the words in Scripture were collected—again in alphabetical order; *Niv Sfatayim,* a very flowery compendium of model letters; *Aspaklaria ha-Meira,* a kind of talmudic encyclopedia; and, of course, *Seder ha-Dorot,* for which I felt a special sort of affection, since its author was a rabbi in nearby Minsk.

Naturally Father's library contained the books of Rabbi Lippa of Mir who had been the *sandek* at my *brit.* His books were on the special half-shelf set aside for the works of authors Father knew personally. Here you found scholarly brochures by rabbis living in the vicinity—they used to bring them carefully wrapped in handkerchiefs. And here on this same shelf stood the commentary on Genesis composed by Rabbi Aaron Katznelson, Grandfather's friend and confidant. Impressive looking despite his blindness, Rabbi Aaron was the first writer I ever met, and I found it astonishing that a man whose book was in our library walked about in the market like anyone else. Though he had been exiled from Moscow along with the rest of the Jews living there, it was to none other than Czar Nicholas II that he dedicated his biblical commentary—finding no one more appropriate, it seemed.

There was a prayer book on the special half-shelf, too—the unique Siddur prepared for the press by Reb Jacob Meir of Minsk, a saintly *Mitnaged* who was deeply disturbed by the thought that the Holy Name was liable to be trodden underfoot or otherwise desecrated whenever a page of an ordinary Siddur fell on the floor. Very carefully, therefore, he had set out pages of a Siddur where the letters of the Name were scattered and printed on a slant so that even if the page became loose and dropped out there would be no desecration. I remember Reb Jacob Meir coming to our town to find subscribers for the new Siddur. My teacher at the time, Reb Bonya by name, called upon us children to help by escorting Reb Jacob Meir to the homes of wealthy townsmen, whose names appeared on a list prepared in the *Bet Midrash*. Reb Bonya assured us that this Siddur would save the world from a fearful sin which impeded the coming of the Redemption. I remember

Reb Jacob Meir as a tall, thin old man wearing a black velvet hat and a long robe that reached to the top of his shoes; he walked along with me, splashing in the mud, while his lean, yellowish hand shielded his eyes to keep him from looking at that forbidden sight—a woman.

On the shelf with Reb Jacob Meir's Siddur there was later to stand a partial Commentary on Maimonides' *Guide to the Perplexed* by another one of my teachers. It was by Reb Yerachmiel Greenberg, a marvellous auto-didact and philosopher who, living in the obscurity of Turetz and of a village near Yirmitch, composed a Hebrew-Arabic dictionary which he hoped all his life to see printed and never did. In addition he composed a large commentary on Maimonides, of which only one small part was published; he kept the matrices hopefully on his shelves all his life, but to no avail. If the crown of authorship escaped him, the crown of a martyr's death was his. During the days of Hitler, he was murdered with all the community of the town of Gorodzia.

Were there books of the modern Hebrew Haskalah literature in the library? They were few and chosen at random, but indescribably attractive to me. I remember the collection called *Liviat Hen*, issued by Javetz as a supplement to a newspaper of his. How attractive the pages were in their ornamental borders and how wonderful were the stories of spirits and legends! The first literary collection acquired for the household was a yearbook—Nachum Sokolow's *Sefer ha-Shana* for 1900. I read and reread it avidly and found endless interest in it. It occupied a place of honor near Joshua Steinberg's Russian-Hebrew Dictionary. Near it stood the utterly delightful little verse anthology *Kinor Zion,* Poems of Zion, most of which I knew by heart. One day I learned from a yeshiva student, the *"Molestoiker,"* how to write Hebrew script as tiny as the Russian letters which had once been used by the youngster who wrote the Russian hymn "God Save the King" on a grain of barley and sent it to the Czar. Then I ran home and wrote one of the poems in the *Kinor* in the shape of a tiny Star of David which I presented to my beloved Zionist uncle.

Near the *Kinor* there was the cherished, thick, little volume of Ben-Avigdor's short stories, *Sifrei Agur.* I was positively intoxicated by those simple direct narratives about Leah the fishwoman, about the wise carpenter and the others—there were whole worlds in those pages of tiny print.

A corner of my own books was beginning to develop in the library—Aaron Rosenfeld's *Gan Shaashuim*; Berman's *Mi-Giborei ha-Uma*; Kalman Shulman's *Harisot Betar*; A. Z. Rabinowitz's history, *Toldot Yisrael*; and Chaim Zvi Lerner's grammar, *Moreh ha-Lashon,* inside of which was the table of verb forms that I studied. Taviov's anthology, *Miv-*

har ha-Sifrut, was added later, and for a while the shelf held Weiss' history of the talmudic sages, *Dor Dor ve-Dorshov;* this was a birthday present from Father, bought in Halprin's book store in Minsk, but when Grandfather caught sight of the volumes, he sighed deeply, took them out of the bookcase and hid them somewhere.

There was none of the literature of talmudic *pilpul* in Father's library, for he bought only what he was personally interested in. When I had to prepare my bar mitzvah sermon, under the guidance of our relative, the Slabodka-trained Reb Elya Tamarkin, the latter was eager to have me use *Shaagat Arye* and *Amudei Or.* Neither was to be found in Father's library nor anywhere else in the town, and I had to get them from Grandfather's large collection at his home in Mir.

My mother had a special section for her books. Though she read both Hebrew and Russian, her religious books were in old Yiddish—*Reshit Hochma* and a very thick *Zeena u-Reena,* printed in a special type somewhat like Rashi script and decorated with fascinating pictures. She had *Nofet Zufim* there and *Kav ha-Yashar* and *Menorat ha-Maor,* and pamphlets of *Maase Alfes* which were very new but nevertheless already established on her shelf. Then there were the books she constantly used: prayer books and the Five Books of Moses; *Mahzorim* for the High Holy Days; Psalters; the *Ethics of the Fathers;* special services (*Tikkunim*) for midnight—*Tikkun Hatzot*—and Shevuot and Hoshanah Rabba; Lamentations for Tisha b'Av; *Selihot* prayers; illustrated copies of the Passover Haggadah for every member of the household; a Purim scroll of the Book of Esther; a calendar; a book of horoscopes; a letter-writing manual; a minature booklet of the Grace After Meals. Books in foreign languages came next—volumes of the Russian Jewish magazine, *Voschod*; an illustrated volume of *Ost und West*; a novel by the famous German writer, Spielhagen; a large volume of the Yiddish magazine *Hausfreund*; and stray books which belonged in either Uncle's library or my sisters'. (I can remember neither the names of those books nor the order in which they were arranged.)

On top of the bookcase inside a special wrapper there were unbound pamphlets of *Divrei Elohim Hayim*. These accounts of hasidic preaching were brought from the rabbi's house by Grandfather when he returned from Ladi or by the emissary who paid us a visit every year. Grandfather used to study the pamphlets with Father, while I sat by and listened. Those rounded, pearly letters running along arched lines engraved themselves on my mind forever.

In a special corner at the other end of the top shelf was kept everything pertaining to the Land of Israel. There was a tiny little book with a "heart" pasted on it and a Hebrew map inside, depicting the route the tribes took through the wilderness on their way from Egypt to the Land; alongside each tribe's camp was its special flag. Then there was Judah Grazovsky's lovely little *Eretz Yisrael* and a book called *Eretz Hemda* and a brochure by Slutzky about the Hibat Zion Movement, and all the letters received before every festival from Tiberias and Safad and Hebron, along with receipts from Jerusalem and drawings of the Wailing Wall and of Rachel's Tomb flanked on both sides by olive trees.

At the end of that top shelf, alongside the wall, stood a cherished possession of ours that was not a book but had such importance and sanctity as fully to deserve a place in the bookcase. This was the silver filigree Hanukkah lamp, presented as a wedding gift to my parents by my great-grandfather. It had eight tiny pitchers for oil, a back that was all flowers and blossoms, and two slender stalks branching out on both sides of the *shamash* candle. All year long the lamp was enclosed in a cardboard box tied with black string, and inside that same box Father kept his Zionist *shekel*.

For me this library of Father's was more precious than anything else in our household. Though I did not then know what was in the books, I knew their savor, their fragrance; even in the dark I could guess the exact place of each book—in the bookcase and in my heart. So when on the eve of Passover I was asked to help air the library, I felt as if I had been invited to participate in some sacred rite. Like a skillful artisan taking a large complicated machine apart down to its smallest screws in order to reassemble it, I would move book after book down from the shelves, only to return them eventually to their places—reuniting the limbs into a single, whole, and beloved organism.

The Maggid
of Minsk

☆

I was born too late to hear the great preachers —the *maggidim*—whose fame lived in all the Jewish communities of Lithuania. The outstanding ones of my own time never came to Steibtz. The *Hasidim* in the *shtiebel* had little use for preaching, and only mediocre *maggidim* appeared in the Old Synagogue of the *Mitnagdim*. My teacher, the *parush* of Koiden-hove, who was the father of the renowned *maggid*, Reb Elyakim Getzel of Brisk, occasionally spoke to me about his noted son, but the stories he told me were full of sadness—it grieved him greatly that

Reb Elyakim had deserted a life of study for preaching and he was bent upon saving me from a similar fate. My "running after the preachers" would turn me into an ignoramus, he threatened.

I was, in fact, so enchanted with *maggidim* that I listened to them avidly, and from a very early age repeated every sermon to my father at the dining room table. I reproduced even the tune and the gestures. Then I began to compose my own sermons, wrapping a sheet around myself in imitation of a preacher's prayer shawl, and piling stools on each other to serve as a pulpit. I would get the whole family together around the table and proceed to deliver my sermon, based usually on verses of Isaiah or Proverbs, both of which I knew by heart. The biblical sentences were interspersed with the few talmudic stories I had picked up in my Gemorra studies, and I would harangue my audience, clearing up difficult points like a real *maggid*, and making up my own parables.

I remember only a few of the traditional *maggidim* who appeared in Steibtz. There was the blind *maggid* who used to come during the days of *Selihot* and preach in the Old Synagogue after midnight when the prayers for forgiveness were said. I had to plead with Father over and over again till at last he agreed to wake me up and take me along. And then I saw the dark, young, sightless *maggid*, standing there lean and tall, as the dawn rose, and pleading with our Heavenly Father in a thin, lyrical voice, drenched with the grief of all the generations.

I recall, too, a plump *maggid* whose family name was Hecht (i.e., pike), and whose favorite subject was the fate of fish. He would describe in excessive detail the sorrow of the fish writhing under the merciless housewife's knife as she prepared her Sabbath dinner. All women, including the most saintly, he insisted, enjoy cutting a live fish into pieces. Then he would launch into a dialogue between fish and housewife, a long, dramatic dialogue, full of moral sentiments and references to the Talmud. It was all a symbol for the people of Israel whose sufferings failed to stir the hearts of even the most righteous individuals among the nations.

Then there was a *maggid* whose name I do not remember though I am indebted to him for the first lesson I ever had in Jewish history—a vivid and terrible description of the working of the Spanish Inquisition. Later in my childhood I was to read books about our people's sufferings in exile—Friedberg's *Vale of Cedars*, Steinberg's *In Those Days,* Mordovitz's *Between Hammer and Anvil*—but all of them were only a continuation of what I had heard from that wonderful preacher who first impressed the fact of Jewish martyrdom upon my heart.

A *maggid* whom I knew very well was Steibtz' own Reb Iche Tanhums, famed among us for the sweet tune in which he chanted his sermons and the lovely parables he included in them. Reb Iche taught Bible to the children of the town's enlightened families, was instructor in *Ein Yaakov* at the Craftsmen's Synagogue, and used to recite chapters from the Book of Job in the homes of mourners. Each time I saw him go up on a platform to speak, I was overwhelmed by the miraculous change in his appearance: his face shone, his eyes lit up, his voice seemed to begin singing by itself. Yet this was the same Iche Tanhums whom we all knew so well and whose piety was rather suspect in our most orthodox circles. When he spoke, all this was forgotten and his hearers sat glued to their places, hanging on every word, no longer individuals but a single body.

I was a child when the *maggid* of Minsk spoke in Steibtz. The circumstances which brought him to us are somewhat vague in my mind, but the melody of his words lives in my heart, plaintive and tremulous, rising and falling, bringing a whole world to life. . . .

A great rabbi had died—I cannot recall whether it was Rabbi Yitzhak Elhanan Spector of Kovna or Rabbi Yehoshua Leib Diskin of Jerusalem. At any rate, the grief in the Old Synagogue was overpowering. Our rabbi delivered a eulogy, as did the rabbi of the neighboring town. But the community was not content until special arrangements were made to bring the *maggid* of Minsk to eulogize the illustrious man who had died.

On the platform in the packed synagogue stood a bearded man of about forty, wrapped in a *tallit*, speaking with a leonine voice, his eyes pools of water. "*Morai ve-rabbosai*" (My teachers and my masters), the sobbing voice began, instantly enveloping us all in profoundest mourning. One story grew into another, one parable into the next. The language was colloquial and picturesque, sprinkled with Russian words and popular expressions and argumentative phrases which were at once absorbed into the town's thinking and were constantly repeated for many a year. The central theme was a dramatic dialogue between our grief-stricken community and the spirit of the great rabbi whom we were mourning and who was represented as visiting us at that very moment. First the *maggid* took the part of the rabbi, representing him as a stern and loving father, who pleaded with us to leave our wicked ways, mend our conduct, and purify our thoughts, so that he might find it possible to intervene on our behalf before the throne of the Almighty. And then the *maggid*, wailing like a repentant child, became the community speaking to the spirit of the departed. He described all the sorrows of our generation, the troubles of the time, the wiles of Satan; he begged and insisted that the great spirit make his way to the gates of mercy, fall at the feet of our Father in Heaven, prostrate himself before Him and not desist till God felt pity for His people Israel and sent the true Redeemer to them.

Woven into this dialogue was a discourse on the value of tears shed by Jews assembled together, and on the purging power of weeping and the grace that is in pity; and a story as well, a fearful story of a great man who was lost in a snowstorm one winter night and came into the house of a poor Jew who had no refreshments of any sort for the famished guest. What did the poor man do? He lit the samovar and saved his guest from the cold with a glass of hot tea. And now a great man in Israel had come to us from the World of Truth and we were empty-handed, without Torah and without good deeds; evil winds were blowing and a driving storm of apostasy. The great visiting spirit searched for some ground to enable him to plead for Israel, and we could honor him only with tears. "I will furnish the fire and you the water, and we will refresh our visitor."

Suddenly the *maggid* jumped up, tore open the doors of the Holy Ark, thrust his head among the sacred scrolls and cried out bitterly: "Master of the world, how long wilt Thou hide Thy face from us? Rise up now and show mercy to Zion—for the time has come to have pity upon her, the appointed season is here."

And the whole great assembly in the synagogue

—old and young, the women in their special place and all the men—burst into a storm of weeping, and the building was filled with awe and trembling.

I have lived through so much since that day that very few of my childhood emotions have survived unchanged. But I still hear that weeping just as it was and I still remember how it felt to weep with all the others.

Years afterwards when I heard Hannah Rovina in Pinsky's play crying beside a wall on the night of the Destruction, that lament of hers seemed to me akin to the weeping in the synagogue, and when I read Bialik's phrase "My heart, a vessel full of tears," my first association was the *maggid* of Minsk.

I remember that the town insisted on asking the *maggid* to stay another day. He consented and preached again, this time after morning prayers. With signs and portents, with logical argument and analysis, with dramatic and picturesque effects like those of the night before, he proved beyond any shadow of doubt that the Torah was given on Mount Sinai, that Israel was the chosen people and that the Redeemer would of a certainty come. For all of us what he said was illuminating and clear, definite and infinitely consoling.

After that morning I never saw the *maggid* again and never heard anything about his sermons. Our ways were too far apart. Many decades later reading a description of life in Soviet Russia, I learned that the Yevsektzia* had made the *maggid* of Minsk a favorite target of their anti-religious activity. He had been arrested and forced to sign his name to some document on Yom Kippur. Over all the distances between us his anguish became mine.

Suddenly one day I came on an item in the newspaper to the effect that every Friday night in a certain Tel Aviv synagogue the *maggid* of Minsk preached on the bibical Portion of the Week. It was hard to believe that he was still alive and even harder to believe that he was among us and that one might hear him in Tel Aviv. More than once I resolved to go to see him, but somehow I never could.

Then one day on a Tel Aviv street I saw a black-bordered announcement that the *maggid* of Minsk had died and memorial tributes would be paid to him on a certain day in a certain Tel Aviv synagogue by a number of rabbis. . . . I stood there, unable to move. When the day came, I found myself involved in a long meeting dealing with pressing problems of the moment. But when the hour for the memorial assembly approached, I simply got up and left. All the way to the synagogue, I kept reproaching myself for never having found time to talk with the old man and learn how he felt about us in this Zionist endeavor of ours, how he felt about everything his eyes saw in the Land he had reached at the end of

* The Jewish section of the Communist Party, entrusted with rooting out anti-Communism or heresy among Jews.

his days. Had he become reconciled to our ways and given his blessing? Or had he raged and cursed?

One thing I was sure of: that whether he knew it or not, he had a share, no mean share, in it all. In any perceptive reckoning of the sources from which our pioneers drew their courage and determination, the *maggid* with the heart that was a "vessel of tears," must surely be included. For over half a century he bore his message through the towns and villages of Lithuania and Russia, and many were the children who, listening to him in their formative years, absorbed into their own hearts his love of Israel, his lamentation over the sorrows of Israel, his faith in the future of Israel. They carried these within them—until they could no longer remain tranquilly in their places and became builders of their nation here.

I reached the synagogue designated in the announcement—I really had not known that such imposing buildings for religious purposes were to be found on obscure side-streets in Tel Aviv. It was absolutely full—the women's gallery as well as the men's section. The men, to be sure, were of a type familiar to anyone who walked on the streets of Tel Aviv, but they always seemed insignificant exceptions in that modern environment and among so many young people. Here, where they were all together with no outsiders about, all of them with long beards, many with sidelocks and a large number with long *capotes*, you forgot that you were in Tel Aviv. It was Lithuania, a small town like my own in Lithuania, that you were inevitably brought back to by their wrinkled faces, their loose strands of hair, their obvious poverty, their Yiddish speech.

On the platform a *maggid* stood, a relative, I was told, of the *Natziv*, the famous head of the Volozhin Yeshiva. The melody of his chant was the same—or at least of the same family—as that I had heard from the *maggid* of Minsk—trilling, penetrating the depths of the soul, penitent and pleading, scolding and moaning, and completely conquering the hearer's heart. And the text was the same: "Mourn me warmly for I shall be with you." And then the same sort of dramatic dialogue between the Jewish people drowning in a sea of troubles—new, realistic troubles—and the faithful, beloved envoy sent to plead before our Father in Heaven. The envoy this time was Reb Binyamin, the *maggid* of Minsk himself. Then suddenly the *maggid* sprang up, tore open the doors of the Holy Ark, thrust his head among the sacred scrolls and cried out bitterly: "Master of the world, how long? How long wilt Thou forget the flock of Thy pasture? Rise up now— have mercy on Zion. . . ." And all the assembly, above and below and from the sides of the hall, burst into tears.

The same storm of weeping. . . .

I turned my head and saw, beside me, next to a
bench, a boy of eight or nine, clearly overwhelmed
by emotion, his large, shining eyes fixed immovably
upon the lips of the *maggid*.

My First
Poet

☆

Examine all your spiritual and intellectual values and you will find that invariably, the first seed was sown somewhere far away in the blessed field of childhood. How, then, can I write of my childhood without acknowledging the great debt of thanks I owe to that gifted and tragic youth, the first poet I ever met, whom I marvelled at and loved with all my soul, who first implanted in me love of Hebrew and Hebrew literature, poetry and poets?

Yaakov Shalom Katzenelenbogen was the name of this meteorlike young poet who from his obscure, little town soared into the skies of literature. His pen name—composed of his initials—was Yashak, and in our town we called him Dadel.

In Israel before World War II, if you ever asked any young immigrant from Steibtz who his Hebrew teacher at home had been, you were sure to be told, "Alter." Alter Yosselevitz was in fact the first to give Hebrew lessons in dozens of homes and then to set up a school where Hebrew was the only language used. Later, he transferred his school to the Tarbut network, found supporters and trained assistants, and brought up the whole of the Hebraist generation of Steibtz. His opponents were many: first the fanatical rabbi and his coterie, then the various types and factions of Yiddishists. But in his Hebrew school Alter succeeded in imbuing scores upon scores of students with love of Hebrew and love of the Land of Israel. He was fortunate enough to see many of his pupils make their way to the Land and to have his own children, Hebrew-speaking from childhood, become teachers there. He and his beloved wife, with the students then in his school, were sacrificed upon the altar of annihilation on that day of vast slaughter when all the Jews of Steibtz, thousands of them, met their deaths at the hands of the Nazis. . . .

But my childhood days in *heder* preceded Alter's coming to the town. When he arrived, I was already president of the Hebraist Children's Zionist

Society, Zion u-Sfata (Zion and its Tongue). We took it upon ourselves to find pupils for Alter and so keep him in the town. During my own early *heder* years there was no one in Steibtz to teach Hebrew as a language. Isser, the son of Yonah the winemaker, an eccentric and solitary old bachelor, was said to be a fine Hebrew stylist, but he was too unstable to be entrusted with young children. Old Yonah himself served as representative of Hebrew grammar in the *shtiebel*: during the reading of the Torah on Saturday mornings he busied himself with discovering brilliant annotations in Ibn Ezra's commentary, pointed them out to my young uncle, and entered into deep discussions, delightful to both of them, concerning fine points of grammar. The deaf old Koidenhove *Hasid* who was head of the *shtiebel* would hush him angrily: "Nu, nu! *Kriat ha-Torah!*" (The Torah is being read!) I must admit that Reb Yonah's enthusiastic and learned dialogues were completely unintelligible to me, for none of my teachers had as yet instructed me in even a single rule of grammar.

When it came to the Hebrew of the Bible, there was a more legitimate and gifted "representative" in the person of Reb Iche Tanhums, who taught Bible in our town and was a *maggid*—itinerant preacher—outside of it. I had friends who studied with him and I was always eager to hear from them how sweetly and melodiously he explained biblical verses. And I found it hard to tear myself away from the homes of mourners, where Reb Iche would be asked to read and explain the Book of Job. Facing the orphans who were bent over on their little stools, he would chant sadly: "Let the day perish wherein I was born, And the night wherein it was said: 'A man-child is brought forth!'" Then, taking as his text that perplexing verse in Ecclesiastes: "It is better to go to the house of mourning than to go to the house of feasting," he would describe the difference between the two with convincing concreteness, analyze what the two had in common, and set forth the vanity of vanities in man's supposed pre-eminence. It was a dissertation that broke the hearts of all his hearers. But Grandfather was on guard lest I fall into Reb Iche's snare. And I did not fall. . . .

So it was that I studied only Bible and Gemorra, and—to my father's great regret—absolutely no grammar.

This was the state of my education until there appeared in our town the teacher Dadel, who was the writer and poet Yaakov Shalom Katzenelenbogen, later to publish verse and prose in David Frischman's *Ha-Dor* under the name of Yashak, and stories and essays in *Ha-Degel* of London.

Katzenelenbogen was the youngest son of the old rabbi in the tiny, nearby town of Svirzna. He had led a revolt of students in the *mussar*-dominated

yeshiva of Reb Yayzel in Novahruduk and then fled
from the yeshiva.

Even Grandfather could not object to my studying with Katzenelenbogen. His older brother was a
famous prodigy, and was later to succeed their
father as rabbi in Svirzna. The oldest brother was a
supervisor in the Mir yeshiva, and the father, one of
the most respected rabbis in the region, a fine old
man, was a close friend of Grandfather's and deeply
respected by Mother. Dadel, for all his rebelliousness
and eccentricity, was the delight of his old father,
and known to be a wonder child—master of both
Torah and modern learning. He simply could not
be rejected.

To be sure, it was inconceivable that I be taken
out of the hands of my teacher, the *parush*, and entrusted to the young Katzenelenbogen. But in the
summer the opportunity came. Year in and year
out my mother and sisters spent the hot months in
the dense wood of Ataliz which was full of pines,
birches and nut-trees, cherries and mushrooms. The
wood belonged to our wealthy uncle and served as
a summer resort for all branches of the family. Every
summer up to then I had stayed at home with Father
so as to keep on studying in the *heder*, and the two
of us had joined the family in the wood only for the
Sabbath. This year my sisters agreed to study Hebrew in the summer, and young Katzenelenbogen

was taken along as tutor. Since he was there and available to me, and my health was not too good, it was decided to take me out of school for a month and send me to convalesce in the wood.

The old rabbi of the town, Reb Shlomo Mordecai Brodni, could not reconcile himself to the idea that I was to study Hebrew grammar with a rebellious yeshiva student, even if that student was Dadel. He tried to persuade Mother to give up the dangerous plan, but this time he failed—she had already given her word to the rabbi of Svirzna. In a final attempt to weaken the evil influence to which I would be exposed, he asked Mother to have me come to see him before I left for the wood.

I can still remember the conversation between the stern, seventy-year-old rabbi, author of a volume of Responsa called *Ohel Shem*, and my ten-year-old self. The rabbi lay on a sofa among the books in his study, and the child stood beside him. The rabbi said something like: "Zamke, do you think Gordonke* knew Hebrew?"

"Rabbi," I said, "I haven't read any of Gordon's poems yet."

"Then listen to me, my child. I have read his poems and I tell you that he knew the Holy Tongue as well as the great writers of *Piyut* you read in the

* Yehuda Leib Gordon (1831-1892), leading Hebrew poet of the Enlightenment in Russia. The diminutive is deprecatory.

Prayer Book. But Gordonke will rot away before any one will put anything of his in the holy Siddur! Why? Because just knowing the Holy Tongue isn't enough. First of all you must fear God and observe His commandments—and after that it is good to know grammar, too. Of course it's good. It is a religious duty to know grammar accurately. But only if you are taught grammar by God-fearing men and remain God-fearing yourself after learning grammar. You understand me?"

With this he dismissed me, and I went off to the care of the son of the rabbi of Svirzna who, driven by the whirlwind of a generation in revolt, had fled from Reb Yayzel the *mussarnik's* yeshiva and became a teacher of Hebrew and a poet writing Hebrew verse for the journals of the Hebraists.

There is much to tell some other time about the wood of Ataliz and the blessings of nature which it lavished suddenly and generously upon a child brought up in town and captive in the *heder*, a child who discovered new instincts here and the first blissful glimmer of love. But now it is the magic of the first encounter between the child and a living Hebrew poet that must be described.

The life of our town as I knew it had not prepared me to meet a poet. The prophets of the Bible were divine and distant, while the poems my sisters talked about so enthusiastically were in Russian and meant nothing to me. As for modern Hebrew poetry, not even a faint echo of it had reached our home.

Yashak was a modern poet, and he wrote in Hebrew, a language which no one around me spoke. His poetry was full of pictures and deep emotion, and when the creative spirit seized hold of him he became intoxicated with his own verse. I cannot forget my amazement when one day as we were walking along the green path from our cottage to the hill deep in the wood, his eyes lit up with a fire I had never seen before and he began to declaim line after line—new, splendid lines which he had just composed, joined to each other, rhythmic and singing and marvellously rhymed as if to herald and confirm each other.

Yashak was tall and had a sharp profile and the strong expression that comes with will-power and abundant imagination. As the youngest child of old parents, he was said to have been very much spoilt. His mustache was just beginning to grow, and above his warm, brown eyes his forehead was very high and steep and intellectual. Because of the part he wore on the left, his black hair covered the upper right side of his forehead. "An original and very interesting head," the girls of the town used to say.

It was with the girls that he spent most of his time, even though the daughters of our good families were generally not interested in Zionists and Hebraists. The dividing line between Zionists and non-Zionists had already begun to be clearly marked, and cultivated girls who spoke Russian and prepared for examinations were almost all on the other side of the line, along with the visiting students, the externe-teacher, and, in time, the Bundist workers. Yashak blurred the line. He was ready to give his soul for Zionism; Hebrew literature—what he had brought with him from clandestine reading in the yeshiva and what he wrote himself during sleepless nights—was the essence of his life. And yet all the girls who were his friends spoke Russian and prepared for examinations. . . .

That summer my sisters, who were already far from Zionism and Hebrew, studied selections from the Bible and Hebrew poetry with Yashak, while he began to teach me the rules of grammar according to C. Z. Lerner's book. I would walk along the long row of evergreens reciting: "*Kusav, nichtav, kittav, koottav, hichtiv, huchtav, hiskatav.*" Up and down the row, back and forth.

It was during that summer that Yashak explained to me enthusiastically and in minute detail the great changes transpiring among Jews since the appearance of Theodor Herzl and the establishment of the Zionist Congress. He spoke to me as if I were a grown-up friend of his, most of those conversations taking place on Friday afternoons in the woods while he was trimming his beard under a tree. To do this in the house where my mother might see him was obviously impossible, and so I would bring him a mirror and hold it up for him while he shaped his beard and talked at length about the history of the Jewish people and its future in Zion. He would talk also about the great men leading the Zionist movement and those who were creating the prose and poetry of the Hebrew renascence: from him I heard for the first time the names of the writers Micha Joseph Berdichevsky and Saul Tschernichovsky, both of whom he admired enormously.

Then, too, I heard the story of the revolt he had taken part in at the *mussar* yeshiva of Novahruduk: the long, fearful *Shaa* the angry students had hissed in unison one night, never stopping till Reb Yayzel, the ascetic head of the yeshiva, and his assistants fled in panic. Reb Yayzel had persecuted every student with Zionist learnings and his supervisors searched the boys' rooms for modern Hebrew books hidden in their boxes. Yashak raged as he spoke of the teachers that stunted the spiritual growth of talented yeshiva students who might give so much to the Jewish people. There was something here of Bialik's passionate cry in *ha-Matmid*. A whole new world of deeply disturbing problems opened before me.

Though I did not know Reb Yayzel and had never studied among *mussarniks*, I relived the storm of the students' protest as my beloved tutor communicated it to me; in my mind's eye I saw Dadel among his enraged companions, hissing into the night at the yeshiva. For me that *Shaa* assumed some of the glory of a manifesto.

When I grew older and came upon the thin, precious pamphlets of Berdichevsky's searing writing, it semed to me, as I devoured his words, that I was listening to a continuation of my poet-teacher's conversations with me in the wood of Ataliz. The *Shaa* he had organized against the ascetic Reb Yayzel, the verses he composed, and the pamphlets of Berdichevsky all merged into a single intimation of a new springtime.

When the summer was over, Dadel travelled to Pinsk where he spent the winter with his mother's family. During the next summer he again spent much of his time with us. He was an even more ardent Zionist now and a more practiced writer.

Whenever he stayed overnight, he brought a little valise with him. And I knew what was in the mysterious case—manuscripts, his delight and mine.

I was still only his pupil. My older sisters were much closer to him and he was with them a great deal. Even then I sensed the pathos of the fact that his writings and poems—dearer to him than anything else—were not for their ears, since they knew no Hebrew. I was beginning to understand the spiritual alienation from women friends that was the "natural" fate of the Hebrew poet in foreign lands.

It was in Yashak's hands that I saw *Ha-Shiloach** for the first time. I was too young to appreciate the periodical, but I understood very clearly how precious it was to my teacher, how close to his heart the poem by Bialik in that issue was and the essay by Ahad Ha-Am and the *feuilleton* of "Rabbi Kariv" (E. L. Levinsky). The thin, green magazine in my teacher's quivering hand became for me a counterweight to the cold, alien Russian monthly, *Obrazovania*, tucked so confidently under my oldest sister's arm. And I was already certain on which of the scales I myself would be weighed.

All my fellow townsmen still alive in Israel remember the fervor with which Yashak leaped into the battle for the sale of Colonial Bank shares. When a well-known Zionist orator, J. L. Berger, came from Minsk to urge us to buy shares, the rabbi would not permit him to speak in the Old Synagogue; even the fact that he was the son of Reb Gershon Abraham, close friend of the rabbi, did not help. Zionist influence being stronger in the New Synagogue, the controversial meeting was held there, but the rabbi's faithful followers—the "Cossacks of the Almighty," as they were called in the town—were not daunted. The moment Berger stood up on the platform, they began to beat on the desks of the *stenders* in front of them, making such a din that it was impossible

---

* Hebrew literary monthly edited by Ahad Ha-Am.

for him to speak. It was at this moment that Dadel jumped up to the platform determined to save the situation. With all the ardor of his heart and all the strength of his voice, he outshouted the noise and began to explain who Berger was and what the Bank was and what the shares meant. He seemed to be "stilling the people," when in the midst of his enthusiastic speech he had the bad fortune to use the still unfamiliar word "Orthodox" in the plural form "Orthodoxen." This was to much for Shaul the keeper of the bathhouse, a leader among the rabbi's disciples. Enraged, he rushed to the platform and screamed: "Did you hear what that *shkotz*, that young heathen, dared to call us? 'Oxen,' he says we are! We're not surprised—we've known for a long time that he's a complete heretic." No one listened any longer to what Yashak had to say. The case was lost.

About this time his father, the rabbi of Svirzna, died, and his widowed mother married the wealthy old man who headed the Koidenhove *Hasidim* in our town. From then on Steibtz was his town, too, and since he had no real home of his own, our home was his. Even when he was away on his travels—generally, I think, to Pinsk—his mother, the hearty old rebbitzin, spent many hours with my mother. I used to love listening to her stories about Yashak's childhood; how playful he had been and how strong-willed and stubborn, the ruler of the house when he was no more than a little boy. One day Yaakov Shalom came back from *heder*, she said, and announced that he must no longer be called by that name. A new boy from another town had appeared in the class; his name was Dadel, and Yaakov found the name so attractive that he insisted on taking it for his own. When the rabbi's household did not accept the new name, Yaakov went into the kitchen, took the pots off their hooks on the wall, and started to knock them against the table, shouting, "I won't stop till you call me Dadel!" From that day on he was Dadel at home and in school and among all his acquaintances.

He began his literary career in the same rebellious, contentious mood. The first piece of his I ever read was a satire on the town leadership. And the pseudonym he chose playfully then was not Yashak which he was later to use in *Ha-Dor*, but those three initials of his name supplemented by N Y (for *nero yair*, "may his light continue to shine")—all of which amounted to *Yeshakeni*, the "let him kiss me" of the second verse of the Song of Songs.

He was already a romanticist as well in those years. I remember one evening in the woods when a number of friends who knew Hebrew came together in our house and Yashak took out of his treasure chest a story he called "Waters That Stood Overnight"—reminiscences of a night-time childhood experience when he accompanied his father to obtain water for use in baking *matzot*. Suffused with a sense of the festival's sanctity, with affection for his elders, and with the wistful longings of childhood, the story was perfectly constructed, original in style, and utterly captivating.

Upon Yashak's return from one of his many long journeys, he sent me on an odd errand. Eager as I was to do what he asked, I simply could not understand what the meaning of it all was. I was to invite the dressmakers of the town to meet on Friday evening in the home of a member of the Girls' Zionist Society, Bnot Zion; Yashak would speak to them about "The New Way in Zionism" which he had brought with him from Pinsk. To be sure, I was a very Zionist-minded child and myself lectured every Saturday to our children's society, Zion u-Sfata, on Jewish history (using A. Z. Rabinowitz's book and Berman's *Heroes of Our Nation*, with slight additions of my own). But with all my reputation for intelligence, I could not see the connection between Zionism and dressmakers or how there could be a "New Way in Zionism" with special reference only to working girls and not to all Zionists. It was quite beyond me.

This new way in Zionism, the combination of Zionism and socialism, seemed to make it necessary to organize Jewish workers, and a lack of available male workers in our town (our few smiths and tailors and shoemakers were already members of the Bund) compelled Yashak to meet with the dressmakers. All this was never adequately explained to me, for the Russian Army called up Yashak, examined him, and found him fit for service. During that same year he was put into uniform.

I remember the deep sorrow that was felt in our house and throughout the town when Yashak was taken to the Army. That this was no place for him, even the most naive among us understood. He himself understood it very well and after he had tasted the alien life of the Russian camp for about two weeks he simply ran away (readers of Hebrew literature will recall the stories of J. H. Brenner and Gershon Shoffman describing Jewish soldiers in army camps; whether they actually knew each other or not, all the young Hebrew writers of that generation seemed to belong to the same family and to have had very much the same fate).

When Yashak escaped from camp, he came—still in his uniform—straight to our house. He had not given a thought to what might happen to him, but as soon as we learned that he had gone off without leave and that everyone, including the police, had seen him rushing through the streets of the town, we understood the grave danger to which he was exposing himself. The family had not even been able to discuss where best to hide him, when the police appeared; and the police, two Christian constables and their Jewish assistant had not even crossed our threshold, when Yashak jumped through a window and ran out. He fled, and the police raced after him. Panic-stricken, the townspeople watched the young man they were so fond and proud of—this prodigy of traditional and modern learning, so distinguished in his ancestry, his Zionism, his Hebrew poetry— running for dear life down the streets, pursued by two corpulent, armed policemen, who blew their whistles and shrieked: "Catch him! Catch him!" while after them, running and stumbling and ostensibly shouting, trailed the Jewish policeman with the shiny tin badge on his chest. The vague phrase, "running away from the Army," had suddenly become terribly concrete for all us onlookers; it was like a deer fleeing from hunters in a forest.

Naturally no one of all the townspeople so much as lifted a finger to catch the fugitive, but they did nothing to help him either: fear of the authorities was simply too strong. They stood there petrified, staring at the ghastly spectacle. Only the Jewish policeman turned aside for a second and slipped into our house, whispering something to my sister and hastily returning to the chase. A few minutes later my sister handed me her little valise packed with some of her clothing and told me to carry it to the shed in her friend's yard. All this while Katzenelenbogen was still running like an arrow speeding through the air along the synagogue street straight to the market, with the policemen at his heels. In the market place he jumped onto the railing of my uncle's house and from the railing into the courtyard and from the courtyard into the garden, the policemen whistling and shouting after him all the time. And then in the garden he climbed on the fence, jumped up into a tree and then into another tree— and vanished.

Half an hour later Reuvele the waggoner drove his carriage in leisurely fashion through the town. His passengers were three girls: one was my sister; the second, her friend, the daughter of our wealthy man and granddaughter of Yashak's mother's new husband; and between them sat an elegant young lady, dressed like the daughter of a Polish nobleman —with a hat and parasol. Along the synagogue street, then across the Nieman River, the carriage travelled, heading toward the tar furnaces that belonged to our wealthy man.

From those tar furnaces young Katzenelenbogen made his way to the border, and from the border to Lvov, and from Lvov to London. We were never to see him again.

Every once in a while the mail brought a magazine from London to our house, an issue of *Ha-Degel* with a leading article on Zionist matters written by him, or an issue of Fuchs' *Ha-Shavua* containing a story of his. The Zionists of the town would assemble in the home of their leader, Marshak, to drink tea and read the literary creation of the youth who had gone so far away. The veterans of the movement were delighted by the views he expressed on the Zionist Congress or in criticism of the leadership in London, views put forth with all the authority of a doughty Zionist publicist.

And for us, Yashak's one-time pupils who had since grown up, the appearance of each new story or stanza of verse was an occasion for rejoicing. His "Waters" was published then and his story, "A Winter Night," which was so novel in style and approach and was afterwards to be so favorably criticized and gain such renown. Modern Hebrew literature had not yet seen such a sharply realistic and devastating description of life in a great and terrifying metropolis.

Then Frischman, the editor of *Ha-Dor*, began to publish prose poems written by Yashak in Switzerland: *Nitzanim* (Blossoms) and *Anachot* (Sighs). Here again was something utterly new—poetic miniatures in fresh Hebrew, lyrics characterized by clear perception, lovely pictorial quality, and subdued sensitivity. I knew these poems by heart, and all of us cherished their wealth of thought and inspiration —until one day under a new installment of *Nitzanim* a death notice appeared, a mournful announcement by Frischman that the gifted and promising young poet had drowned in a Swiss lake. . . .

We learned later that he had been rowing on the lake with a young woman friend. When a sudden wave overturned the boat, and they were thrown into the water, he saved the girl but himself sank into the depths.

Who was the girl who saw him in his last moments as he sacrificed his life for her? Was his body ever removed from the lake, and if so, was he given a Jewish burial? And is there some identifying mark on his grave? Despite many attempts, I have never succeeded in finding out. I could not even mourn him as I would have wished to. He died a few days after Theodor Herzl and I was so stunned by the first loss that I could hardly react to the second. My sisters, who did not join in the mourning for Herzl, were able to feel most acutely the pain of Yashak's untimely passing. Katya, the second of the four, who was so learned and opinionated, managed to suppress her grief, but Vitya, the third, who was highly emotional and outspoken—she was afterwards an assistant in the Neuro-Psychiatric Institute in Leningrad and died during the siege—Vitya's sorrow knew no limits, and for many years she could not be argued out of her absolute belief that Katzenelenbogen was alive somewhere, having fabricated the story of his death for some hidden political reason. One day the door would open and he would walk in. . . .

Some time after Yashak's death, the Hebrew-speaking society in London, Agudat Dovrei Ivrit, acting upon Brenner's suggestion, issued the won-

derful London story, "A Winter Night" in a special
brochure with a preface by A. L. Biska, who had
known the author during his stay in England. Yashak,
we learned, had almost starved in London and in
desperation had returned to Russia where he was
caught by the police and imprisoned as a deserter.
He had escaped again, fleeing to Germany, where
for meager pay he took care of a blind scholar,
leading him through the streets of Berlin. From
Berlin he moved to Zurich where he wrote the prose
poems Frischman published—and went on to his
death.

Biska, too, was to die in a few years, before he
could carry out his plans to collect and publish
Yashak's writings. And no one has done this yet. . . .

Once in Tel Aviv early in 1930, as the poetess
Rachel and I sat on beach chairs watching the sea,
I told her about Yashak and his poetry and the influence he had on us in our childhood. She had never
heard of *Nitzanim*, the prose poems I praised so
highly, and she urged me to recite whatever I could
remember of them. A sad and lovely passage came
to my mind, ending with a line of melancholy wisdom:

> *Only the dead cannot die; the living all shall
> die. . . .*

I did not know then how deeply impressed she
had been, but more than a year later, on that bitter

day in April, 1931 when we returned from burying her, as she had wished, in Kinneret, and went up to her empty room on the third floor of 5 Bugrashov Street in Tel Aviv, we found in her desk drawer a slip of paper on which a poem called "My Dead" was written, and underneath the title there was a long line in quotation marks:

> "Only the dead cannot die; the living all shall die." Y.S.K.

Ever since then, this has appeared as the last poem in all editions of Rachel's verse. And so this line from the last poems of the first poet who opened my heart to Hebrew literature is linked with the last poem of the first of our modern women poets who opened the gates of the new Hebrew poetry in our land.

Vera Yakovlevna

☆

Was there a craving for beauty in our town? Do I, as I look back upon my childhood, recall a feeling for art? Did the people know what love is?

If I succeed at all in telling the story of Vera Yakovlevna, I shall answer all these questions and many more, for I shall be describing the festive atmosphere, the splendor and intoxication that her presence brought into our town from the day she first appeared in it until the time she vanished.

Vera Yakovlevna was the most beautiful woman I had ever seen, and all the townspeople insisted that they had never known anyone so lovely. She was the wife of the young Dr. Levitan, who had recently been invited to practice in the town. For many years Steibtz suffered from unsympathetic, often non-Jewish doctors who treated their patients insolently and roughly. The younger heads of families had finally succeeded in bringing to the town this thoroughly Jewish physician, Moisei Abramovitz Levitan. They remembered him from his student days when he came from his university in Kharkov one summer vacation to visit his uncle, the doctor in a nearby town. The two had spent a Sabbath in Steibtz and for years afterwards people talked about the young man's goodness and ability, his Jewish loyalty, and how conscientiously he had gone on studying despite his poverty. His uncle, the Dr. Levitan of my early memories, helped him as much as he could, and one day we heard from the uncle that even before finishing his medical course the young rascal had fallen in love with a beautiful Jewish singer whom he heard in the title role of Carmen at the Russian Opera in Kharkov. She left the stage for the poor student's sake, married him, and went with him to all the places where he studied.

When it became known that Moisei Abramovitz had finished his internship and was looking for a place in which to settle, the Jewish community in Steibtz, sick of the alien physicians, offered to pay him three hundred rubles a year in addition to the fees he would receive from patients. When he consented, a pleasant home in the center of town was rented for him, and a ladies' committee prepared and decorated the rooms. One bright, sunny spring morning the new carriage of Avramke the driver stopped near that house. Out of it jumped Moisei Abramovitz, who had by now grown a pointed beard and blond mustache. The tall, graceful woman he helped out of the carriage lifted the little veil of her broadbrimmed hat and looked curiously around her. A small boy and a tiny little girl rushed out, talking gaily to her in Russian. Taking them by the hand, she disappeared into the house with them and their nursemaid.

Odd as the name Vera Yakovlevna seemed to us, it was very quickly known throughout the town. The doctor was everyone's friend, the mainstay of all the sick, but she was the glory of the town—and the delight of all who had any esthetic sense—adding a touch of holiday to the everyday drabness of our lives.

She was quickly forgiven for the ringing Russian we heard her talking. She was forgiven, too, for the attractive way she dressed, though it deviated from the town's standards of modesty. Even her ignorance in Jewish matters only gave rise to kindly laughter, and no one dreamt of complaining about her friendly relationships with the local Russian officials. In fact, everybody enjoyed her unconventionality, and everybody—each in his own way, in accordance with his own temperament and age and standing—adored her.

Most of the songs she sang were Russian or foreign, and she had no accompaniment for there was still no piano in the town. But towards evening when she sat with friends at tea in her home and the sound of her singing voice was heard, windows all along the street were flung open, and everyone with a feeling heart remained motionless at the sill until she finished.

One of the characteristically Jewish things that she quickly adopted and then enriched was hasidic melody. Could some vague childhood memory have made this possible, or was it the response of a sensitive spirit? Whatever the explanation, even the most authentically Jewish among us were deeply stirred when she sang a variation on a hasidic tune; it was, they felt, the expression of their own feelings.

I remember one of the first visits she and her husband paid our family one Saturday. Father himself helped her take off her coat and then hung it up. And when in a manner unfamiliar to me she adjusted her tight-fitting, exquisite vest in front of the little mirror in the vestibule and then handed me her hat and veil with a smile that was full of charm and a radiant movement of her head, I was so ecstatically happy that I did not know where I was.

For Father's sake she consented to sing a hasidic

tune she knew, and she sang it sitting close to the table, her eyes closed in devotion, her snapping fingers accompanying her, as if she were a born *Hasid.* The tune was so appealing, so full of longing and promise, that the heart melted at its sound.

We sang it for years at our Sabbath table and we always called it the "Doctor's Wife's Tune." I remember hearing it once from a yeshiva student who ate with us on Saturdays. He fitted the words of the Psalmist to it: "My soul thirsteth for thee, my flesh longeth for thee." I was literally awe-struck. How had this hermitlike boy selected such a marvellously appropriate text—words which in the first place might have been composed to go with the adored melody of Vera Yakovlevna?

I remember another Saturday, a stormy winter day, when for hours I stood, almost frozen, at the corner of the market and the post office street, waiting for the moment when she would pass on her way from her house to the pharmacist's where she used to go to play cards. When she passed, I would have the chance to doff my hat and say, "*Zdravstvuite.*" (How do you do?)

Then there was the time when our relative, Michael Shemi Horowitz, who was a delegate from Minsk to the Zionist Congresses, came to visit our town. It was after the Zionist Conference in Minsk, and the movement was very much on the upsurge in Steibtz. Michael was not only loved by our family but popular among the townsfolk, well-spoken and always full of Zionist information and inspiration. Equipped with a special list, I was sent out to invite the leading Zionists to meet with him at the house of my uncle Hirschel.

With all of them assembled around him, Michael Shemi sat at the head of the table. Immaculately dressed, his beard cleft in two like that of Nordau himself, he spoke with charm that captivated, with sharpness in debate, vividness in description, and a power of conviction that grew out of the definiteness of his opinions. I remember what he had to say about the goals of the Colonial Bank; about Herzl's plans for diplomatic work in Constantinople; about the Arabs in Palestine—how they believed so implicitly in the return of the Jewish people to Zion that any contracts they drew up with each other stipulated that the transfer of land was good only until the return of the Jews. Michael Shemi talked about Jewish students in Germany who had been completely assimilated and were now returning to their people and even fighting duels to defend Jewish honor. He described the Zionist Congress and its splendor, he expatiated on the grandeur of Dr. Herzl's personality. He was "a spring of never-failing waters. . . ." And many an incidental point was woven into the lecture—a wonderful anecdote about meeting Marco Baruch, the famous Zionist anarchist, in Basel; a verse of Frug's; an acute remark by Dr.

Avinovitzki of Odessa; arrows of devastating criticism
shot at some radical assimilationist in Minsk whom
I did not know, and at some Orthodox anti-Zionists
among us whom I knew very well.

All of us gave Michael Shemi our rapt attention,
and all of us felt a sublime happiness in listening to
him. "All of us" included: Marshak, the pharmacist, who was the leader of the Zionists of Steibtz
and wrote anonymously for *Hamelitz*; my uncle
Hirschel, official chairman of the local Zionist Society; Father, who had recently joined the ranks; the
Hebrew teacher, Alter Yosselevitz, leader of the
Daughters of Zion Club; Lusterman, son-in-law of
one of our wealthy men, who subscribed to the illustrated German Jewish cultural magazine, *Ost und
West*; Noah Barsuk, leader of the youth; Pinya, the
most enlightened of the workers; Ahre, son of the
shochet; Reb Haim Itche, the *melamed*, a veteran
member of the Hoveve Zion; and, in addition, many
women and youngsters. All our Zionist elite.

Suddenly I noticed how Michael Shemi kept
looking in one direction and never shifted his gaze:
he was intent on the somewhat hidden corner where
Vera Yakovlevna sat with her shining eyes fixed on
him. She was close to the table, and her delightfully
triangular chin rested on the closed palm of her hand.
She was all eyes and all lovely understanding. She
drank his words thirstily.

Then I knew why Michael's speech this time

was so magical, and for whom its richness was intended.

I saw and was astounded. And I forgave—and understood very well.

It was soon after this that the Russo-Japanese War broke out and Dr. Moisei Abramovitz, the husband of Vera Yakovlevna, was drafted for medical service in the Army. Before he left, our leading citizens assembled in the spacious courtyard of a wealthy home to be photographed with him "in everlasting remembrance." And, as it has turned out, that photograph, with Moisei Abramovitz and Vera Yakovlevna in the center, surrounded by all the enlightened of Steibtz, is the only collective souvenir left of this Jewish town that has been wiped off the face of the earth. I have seen that picture cherished in homes in many lands where the sons and daughters of Steibtz have been scattered.

During the war Vera Yakovlevna remained in the town, a sad "straw widow," more beautiful than ever, secluded in her home, distant and charming, captivating the imagination of many and entirely absorbed in her own world.

After a while there was talk about a Russian officer, an old acquaintance of hers from Kharkov. He came to Steibtz, stayed at the hotel near the railroad station and often visited her. Then he committed suicide. They said it was for her sake. No one was surprised and there was very little talk about it.

☆

Vera Yakovlevna

In those years of the Russo-Japanese War on the eve of the first Russian Revolution, rival labor movements began to spring up in our town. The conflict was sharpest between the Bund and us Zionists, and the chief battle ground was the library established by the young people of Steibtz. When the struggle became particularly intense the library was split in two, they taking the Russian section, which was "theirs," and we the Hebrew, which was "ours." My older sisters helped with the Russian books, assisting the town teacher of Russian and one or another student or externe* or girl student from Bobroisk. Alter, the Hebrew teacher, took care of our books and I helped him, but our faction had no student of its own. When the atmosphere grew even more hostile and the Poale Zion movement was about to be established, we brought a Russian teacher of our side to the town. A brilliant young externe, dazzling theoretician and orator, he instructed us in socialist Zionism. While he was still among us in Steibtz, he became famous throughout our movement because of his profound articles on "The Static and Dynamic Aspects of the Jewish Situation" which appeared in the serious Zionist monthly, *Yevreiskaya Zhizn*, published in the capital.

Our teacher-orator, with his wavy black hair and impeccable manners, was a distant relative of

---

* A student who had not been admitted to a secondary school but was preparing for the examinations by himself.

the town's wealthiest man—a fact which had helped bring him to us. It was he who made it possible for our movement to find its way into the homes of the rich and the circles of the radical intelligentsia—and even behind the closed doors of Vera Yakovlevna. He was a most consistent idealist, a truly ethical man. In his addiction to extreme vegetarianism, he would not allow us to hang fly paper in our meeting room —flies, too, were living things whose lives were sacred. He knew the work of Michailovsky the idealistic philosopher thoroughly and did not accept Marxian materialism; he lectured brilliantly and knew and loved Russian poetry and literature. Though he came from Smorgon near Vilna, his mastery of Russian was like that of a Russian intellectual. Russian was the language he spoke and lectured in and he knew no Hebrew at all. Idelson, the famous Zionist editor, wrote him encouraging letters, and in his heart of hearts he hoped to rival Vladimir Jabotinsky, whose star was then just rising.

By day he gave lessons to externes and in the evenings taught us the doctrines of the young Labor Zionist movement or wrote his articles and studies. Whatever free hours he had were spent in Vera Yakovlevna's house or walking with her far into the woods that surrounded the town.

Then he founded the branch of Poale Zion in Steibtz, and the greatest gift that he gave it was Vera Yakovlevna's help.

The first thing she did for us was to come to the aid of our library, which was so hard-pressed for funds. She set about arranging for the performance of a Yiddish play. Goldfaden's *Shulamis* was what she chose. The rehearsals lasted all winter, and their charm and novelty conquered the hearts of all the young people close to us whenever they were fortunate enough to be in the hall or near it.

No one was allowed into our meeting rooms during rehearsals. Vera Yakovlevna had strictly forbidden it. She had chosen the actors from among our members and sympathizers, and she herself played the role of Shulamis. I can still hear the sound of her voice in the mournful, angry melody the fair Shulamis sang as, longing for her beloved who had left her, she dismissed one after another of her suitors— "*Aveck, aveck, aveck, aveck, a-ve-ck!*"

The performance suddenly lifted us out of our obscurity and made us the focal point for all lovers of beauty in the town. That was Vera Yakovlevna's gift to the movement. But it was a trifle compared to the enormous, unexpected aid her charm and magicial talent rendered us during what was for us a fatal hour of decision.

It was on the Shevuot holiday. We had arranged a secret assembly in the Zadvoriya wood on the other side of the town. "Patrols" lined the paths to point the way to the meeting place. There among the trees we staged our first ideological debate, with some of us impersonating our opponents. This intellectual fencing was intended to give our members practice in answering the arguments of our many antagonists. The teacher directed the "performance"; he had given me the role of a Bundist spokesman and taken it upon himself to answer for Poale Zion. I had diligently gathered the most telling arguments against Zionism, building a towering structure out of what I heard from my sisters and their friends, teachers and visitors, as well as what I could gather from reading and reflection. When our teacher got up after I finished and eruditely tore down every inch of my structure, leaving nothing of it at all, I was triumphant.

Encouraged by the proven correctness of our ideas, fortified by the truth we possessed, we decided then and there to march out together in our first demonstration. This would be the first time we would reveal ourselves to the town in all our strength.

Our flag flying before us, we marched forth, singing.

When we reached the little bridge over the canal, our patrols informed us that our Bundist opponents had just emerged from the other side of the wood and were also prepared for a demonstration. They were now coming close to the town. They were by far the larger group—they had the workers with them, the sons and daughters of the wealthy families, and the best of the intelligentsia. Compared to them, we were a mere handful, most of us very young. We sensed clearly that this first public appearance of ours would be far from triumphant. They must surely have caught wind of our plans and deliberately organized their counter-demonstration for the same time as ours, in order to point up our shameful weakness.

The disaster seemed unavoidable. We were already marching in procession, and from a distance we heard the echo of their footsteps and the sound of their singing. We were doomed to disgrace.

And then Vera Yakovlevna stepped out of the line, took the flag from the hand of the boy who carried it, and in her clear, powerful, enchanting voice began to sing our Party hymn, "The Oath." All of us sang after her, and when the two processions came close to each other, her voice outsang all theirs. When she came face to face with them, she began the song again. The rest of us and, in fact, almost the entire town, followed her all the way to our meeting room.

Then they said in our movement: The balance is now decidedly in our favor.

When the war was over, Moisei Abramovitz came home. Shortly thereafter, he took Vera Yakovlevna and the two children, who were the delight of their mother's friends, and moved to Chita in Siberia.

In doing this, he removed from Steibtz all the loveliness and youthful gaiety Vera Yakovlevna had brought us.

He removed all this beauty, but in a sense he did not remove it at all. The remembered radiance of Vera Yakovlevna shone undimmed in the hearts of those who had known her. When on their way through life they came upon beauty in a woman, they sought invariably to trace in it sparks of the light of Vera Yakovlevna which had shone upon them in the springtime of their lives.

Forty years after Vera Yakovlevna's departure from Steibtz, I met an old Zionist industrialist who had come to Palestine from that same far-off Chita. I asked him if by chance he knew her. His face lit up suddenly, and in his aging eyes I saw again that magic light she had shed upon us in those years when youth was dawning.

Retribution

☆

"But if you do not heed the word of the Lord your God to observe faithfully all His commandments and laws which I enjoin upon you this day, all these curses shall come upon you and take effect."

DEUTERONOMY 28.15

I think I remember how I became aware of the begininngs of revolt in our town. The first clear sign of the historic storm to come was something I saw in the *shtiebel*: the reaction around the shaky table behind the stove when the strong-minded old Zion-Ber staggered the entire company by reporting that in the Great Synagogue, Isser the water bearer had refused to be called up to the Torah during the reading of the Curses in Deuteronomy. Year in and year out this had been his customary role—but this year he simply got up before the Bible reading began and left the synagogue. They looked for him in every obscure corner of the synagogue courtyard. He was nowhere to be found.

"Simply went out?"

"Simply went out!"

The dismay in the eyes of the old men in the *shtiebel*; the angry annoyance of the more moderate; the little smile that lurked under the mustaches of the younger people—all these were premonitions of tempestuous change.

And we children, who did not begin to grasp the full significance of Zion-Ber's announcement, felt instinctively that Isser had not acted without good reason. Our sympathies were with him, for we found it a frightening experience to hear the dreadful words of the Curses chanted by Reb Eliahu: "Cursed shall you be in the city and cursed shall you be in the country. . . . Cursed shall you be in your comings and cursed shall you be in your goings. . . . The Lord will strike you with consumption, fever, and inflammation, with scorching heat and drought, with blight and mildew. . . ."

Horror of horrors! The words lashed out over and over again like hailstones crashing on a tile roof during a stormy night. Isser used to stand there, shrunken and shaking, crushed by the weight of the blows—sacrificed for the sins of the community.

Curiously enough, while Isser was always called up in the Great Synagogue during the reading of the Curses, in the smaller synagogue on Yurzdike they used to call up Yedidya the water bearer. Whether there was or ever had been any formal connection between that particular synagogue function and the occupation of water bearer, the most menial in our economy, I could not say, but the fact remained that both synagogues did this and that the two water bearers belonged to the most wretched families in the community.

Actually, in all the neighboring towns it was not Jews but peasants from nearby villages who practiced the trade, drawing water from the river to fill the barrels that stood in the vestibules of the houses or in the nearby alleys. In Steibtz, too, many families depended for their water on Fabian, the tall "Sabbath *goy,*" who came every Friday night to remove the lamps from the table and was remunerated with a slice of white *halleh* (on the eve of Passover the community's leaven was "sold" to him in the rabbi's office). In a pinch, the housewives were supplied with water by Hafka the washerwoman, who used to get drunk every market day, vociferously curse the Jews, and kiss the village boys while the whole world looked on.

However, in Steibtz it was traditional that the most respected householders should be served by Jewish water bearers, and the latter were, in a way, included among the religious functionaries who had specific duties to perform for the community and for whom the community as a whole was obligated to provide.

For instance, whenever a wedding took place in a synagogue courtyard and the bride and groom, their parents and the rest of the wedding party were on their way back to the bride's home, musicians preceding them and youngsters running behind, the water bearers with their pails over their shoulders used to come out into the street to meet the gay group. They would put a pail of water in front of the couple and the parents would throw copper coins into the pail, while the whole crowd shouted, "*Mazol tov!*"

If a prosperous visitor came to town for the Sabbath and gave a generous donation when he was called up to the Torah, it was to be expected that the next morning as he was about to go on his way, he would find the water bearer waiting near the carriage, confidently stretching out his hand to receive his due.

And for years it had been the immutable custom in our synagogues to have the heads of the two families of water bearers—Yedidya of the Yurzdike and Isser of the River Bank—stand as witnesses for all of us while the dreadful words of the wrath of God were recited by the reader.

The curse of God seemed indeed to be pursuing these two families.

Yedidya's place in the synagogue was near the

door at the back. The unpleasant odor in his vicinity kept us children as far from him as we could get, but we used to tease his one and only son, Abba, who, poor thing, was even less human and more deformed than his father and had an absolutely expressionless face. "Abba, what prayer are they reading now?" children would suddenly ask him, and he, completely confused, would point at random to a passage in the prayer book which he invariably held upside down.

Isser's family had three branches, all living near each other along the river. His younger brother, Avremel, was a hunch-backed dwarf, whose tiny house, hidden among the yards, was always full of naked children rolling on the floor for want of beds. The servant maids of the rich would not deign to enter the house. Instead, they would bend down to knock on the window pane that was only a few feet above the ground and shout, "Avremel, two from the well and one from the Nieman tomorrow."

In other words, Avremel was to bring two pails of water from the well for washing, cooking and laundering, and one pail of fresh river water for tea.

The third brother, Tevele, was a deaf-mute. He, too, was very tiny, and he "spoke" an unrecognizable language of his own. When the Mishna we studied in *heder* taught us that "minors, fools and deaf persons" were not accountable for their actions, we all commented to ourselves: "Like Tevele." He spent the whole day walking with a yoke over his skinny shoulders carrying pails from the river to the homes of respected householders, and back again from their homes to the river. As he walked, he made strange, loud noises which only veteran residents of the town could interpret. He remained a bachelor for many years, his clothes woefully torn and ragged, until some of our God-fearing women took pity on him and married him off to an aging orphan who spent her days in and out of the poor house. Hinda the Roly-Poly was a puffed up, plump, giggly and utterly unattractive spinster. After their marriage, Avremel built them a little hut near his house: it was even tinier than the house, and Tevele's pail had to stand outside because it was too tall to go through the door.

The most normal and healthy of the brothers was Isser, the oldest. Though his wife was tubercular and his children sickly, he himself was erect and agile—a silent, introspective, lean man, on whose tense, ascetic face there was an expression of angry stubbornness.

Isser was a bitter man and there was bitterness in his faithful, rigid observance of religious precepts.

I can still see him as he stood at the west wall of the synagogue, leaning on the window sill with a worn little Psalter in his hand, reading chapters of the Psalms to himself while the rest of the congregation chanted them in unison. He and they read the same psalms at the same time, but he would on no account be one of the group. His quarrel with the community was too far-reaching and grave. Let all the rest recite together; he, Isser, standing close to them, was alone, immersed in his solitary reading, and his thin, irate, ascetic face seemed to be summoning the community to judgment.

After Isser's sudden exit from the synagogue we began to hear that Reb Eliahu the reader had previously suspected Isser of rebellious tendencies. During the same Bible reading a year earlier, while Reb Eliahu was chanting "Cursed shall you be" and "the Lord will strike you . . . ," he suddenly realized that after each imprecation Isser was whispering: "On *your* head! On *your* head!" But this ingenious formula no longer satisfied Isser, and though he was obviously endangering his livelihood, he left the synagogue before the reading began.

As it turned out, however, his livelihood was not affected.

His eldest son, Binyamin Leib, was becoming known as one of the most gifted students in the Talmud Torah. Isser pinned all his hopes on the promising boy. Binyamin Leib was destined to amaze all who knew him; Binyamin Leib would show all the pampered children of the rich who it was that God had blessed "with a good head"; Binyamin Leib would teach all of them a lesson. They would all come to learn Torah from him, and through his scholarly distinction he would lift his father from the dust. He would talk down to all of them. . . .

With Binyamin Leib's growing success in his studies, Isser grew straighter and prouder, standing near the west window of the synagogue while the Pslams were being recited in the twilight. He was no *Hasid* and never expressed strong feelings as the worshippers in the *shtiebel* did by clapping their hands and snapping their fingers. But his tight little fist swung back and forth, automatically it seemed, to the rhythm of the Psalm he chanted:

For the oppression of the poor,
For the sighing of the needy,
Now will I arise, says the Lord. . . .

It was difficult to decide whether this was a bitter complaint or an angry threat or both at once.

It was not long before Yoshe the Talmud Torah teacher walked over to the west window of the synagogue to ask Isser the water bearer whether he would be willing to send Binyamin Leib to Mir to study in the Talmud Torah "at Reb Zaame's table."

That "table" was more than a class in the Talmud Torah. It was a sort of preparatory course for the great yeshiva, and Reb Zaame was famed far and wide as a masterly teacher. His students were very carefully chosen, and there was in fact a sort of "quota" system according to which each town in the vicinity of Mir was entitled to send a specific number of its most brilliant boys to study with Reb Zaame. This time Reb Yoshe chose Binyamin Leib.

Isser's stern face lit up with joy when Reb Yoshe spoke to him. Would he be willing to send Binyamin Leib to Mir? Certainly he would! What a question! He would pawn all his possessions and go without food in order to send Binyamin Leib to the table of Reb Zaame, exactly as Eliahu the *shochet* had sent his son. It was time all the fine people in the town understood that the Torah had not been given exclusively to them.

Isser began to save pennies for his son's journey to Mir. No less painstakingly than he accumulated money, he made every effort to store up credit for good deeds and to become ever more God-fearing, in order to help his son reach great heights.

There were times when Reb Ahre, who was in charge of the synagogue's philanthropies, found it difficult to make arrangements for the Sabbath for some poor visitor to town: the householder whose turn it was to accept such a visitor might not be in the synagogue just then to take him along to his home. At such junctures, Isser the water bearer would always volunteer to escort the stranger to wherever he was being sent. And I remember how one Thursday after evening prayers I went to the Great Synagogue to visit the students who were preparing to review their week's studies till late at night. I met Isser coming in slowly with his pails of water. He put his yoke and pails down in the hallway and with a cup in his hand went up and down the benches to serve good river water to the young scholars. When they said the blessing before drinking, he responded with "Amen," and his eyes were shut in fervent piety.

Most of all, he delighted in hearing students praise his son. Binyamin Leib was becoming more and more famous among us. His biblical knowledge was remarkable, and he could elucidate even the most difficult verses in Ezekiel or Job, astonishing us all with his interpretations and homilies. Though he was four or five years older than my group (we were nine or ten and he had been putting on *tefillin* for as long as two years), he enjoyed coming to our room between afternoon and evening prayers. He would overwhelm us with the erudite questions he posed and the answers he gave, and we knew that a great preacher was growing up among us.

We felt that he was ashamed of his family, and there was a tacit understanding among us never to mention either of his uncles when he was present. They themselves, Avremel and Tevele, did not approach him when they passed him in the street, nor did he approach them. His relationship with his father was different: the two were secret allies. He understood very well what his father wished him to do, and he was fully determined to do just that—to remove the mark of shame from his family by his scholarly achievement. He would be avenging himself on the youngsters in the street by becoming superior to them and resembling the chosen few in our best families.

His first sermons, as I recall them, had nothing tendentious about them and no social content at all. They consisted of scholarly problems and solutions, and their social significance lay in the fact that they were the work of Binyamin Leib, the son of Isser the water bearer, and the nephew of Avremel, the dwarf, and Tevele, the deaf-mute. And when Binyamin Leib spoke, his listeners and admirers were the children of the chief householders of the town.

I remember a discourse of his on Purim night as we were walking out of the synagogue with our teacher after the reading of the Megilla. Why, he asked, does the Book of Esther say that Haman told Zeresh, his wife, "of the glory of his riches and multitude of his children?" That he revealed the extent of his wealth was reasonable enough, for women generally are not well informed about their husbands' finances. But what of the "multitude of children?" Surely Zeresh must have known how many children she had. But—Binyamin Leib went on to explain in the melody of a veteran *maggid*—the Hebrew word *rov*, translated "multitude," refers not to number but to greatness, as it does in the passage of the Haggadah on how strong and distinguished the people of Israel grew in Egypt.

We youngsters were fascinated by Binyamin Leib's commentary, and I, the youngest in the class, turned to him with the same intonation and said: "Binyamin Leib, I think I have good proof that you are right. In the Psalms we studied what David wrote when he ran away from Absalom his son: 'Lord, how are they increased that trouble me! Many are they that rise up against me.' But we know that it was only from Absalom and a little group of his friends that David tried to escape; he wasn't running away from a large number of enemies. So the words 'increased' and 'many' must surely mean stronger and mightier, not more, than he!"

Binyamin Leib enthusiastically lauded my helpful new interpretation and I, for my part, was delighted by his commendation. The teacher apparently paid no attention to what either of us said.

However, the next day after the reading of the Megilla, he repeated our novel suggestions to a large crowd of listeners and gave each of us credit. I can still remember how radiant Isser's face became as, standing attentively by the window in the synagogue, with his elbow on the ledge and his thumb in his mouth, he heard the praises of Binyamin Leib, his son and redeemer.

From then on, whenever Isser looked at me his

stern expression seemed to soften. A sort of sympathy
began to develop between us, and on one occasion he
went so far as to give tangible expression to this
unexpected tenderness.

In my mother's winter cupboard there was a
large jar of raspberry jam which she prepared in the
woods during the summer for medicinal use among
the poor of the town. She distributed it by the glass
—to a sick child who needed to perspire, to an ailing
woman whose lung had shrunk. There were always
people in distress coming to ask her for some of this
red, sweet delicacy that was believed to restore
health and strength. They called it *labung*. (When I
studied Jeremiah's verse: "Is there no balm in Gi-
lead; is there no physician there; why then is not the
health of the daughter of my people recovered?"—
I interpreted the unusual word "balm" as meaning
labung. And then the passage became completely
clear to me.)

When Binyamin Leib's mother became gravely
ill and Velvel the *feldscher** despaired of her life,
Mother sent a glass of jam with me, since I was
close to Binyamin Leib. It was then that I came face
to face with poverty in all its dark misery. Though
Isser wanted no stranger to see his wretchedness and
generally resented all benefactors, my friendship
with Binyamin Leib made an exception of me: Isser
received me graciously and even escorted me home.

* A "healer" with no academic training.

As we talked on the way, it was possible to sense how
great the disagreement between us was going to be.
For Isser was very much attached to Yoshe the Talmud Torah teacher, who was Binyamin Leib's
master, and Yoshe was one of the rabbi's "Cossacks,"
a fanatical hater of Zionism and Zionists. On the
other hand, my friends and I, members of Zion
u-Sfata, were loyal to the Zionists in town and ready
to carry out whatever they asked us to do.

When the Zionists founded a Hebrew library, we
went from house to house to collect books and we
laboriously moved shelves for them into Yoshke the
carpenter's new house. Then we plunged into prepa-
rations for a Hanukkah evening gathering which was
to help us maintain and enlarge the library as a
center of strength for Zionism in the town.

Forthwith the rabbi laid a ban on the gathering.
And one morning soon after, we found our bookcase
lying in the middle of the street and all our dearly
beloved Hebrew books scattered in every direction.
It was rumored that Yoshe the Talmud Torah
teacher, and Shaul the bathhouse keeper had incited
the rabbi against the Zionist library. The well-in-
formed added that Isser had participated in the evil
deed; some even said that Binyamin Leib had also
taken part.

Whether or not that was so, the relationship
between Isser the water bearer and the rabbi's

young men grew increasingly closer during the year. When the cycle of Bible readings brought us once more to the Curses of Deuteronomy, voices in the synagogue spoke out against calling up Isser. Reb Eliahu the reader solved the problem—he took upon himself the fearful function that had traditionally been Isser's.

This extraordinary happening was the talk of the whole town. Furthermore, when the High Holy Days passed, Yoshe the teacher came to inform Isser that he had made all arrangements for Binyamin Leib to enter Reb Zaame's Talmud Torah in Mir. Isser, making a supreme effort, sent the son he so loved to that admired place of learning. And there, Isser hoped, Binyamin Leib's remarkable scholarship would enable him to throw off the burden of humiliation which had tormented the whole of his wretched family throughout their lives.

Binyamin Leib stayed in Mir for four consecutive terms. When he returned home, the townspeople hardly recognized him, and the town itself was profoundly changed. During those two years Russia had gone through the first stages of its first revolution, and Zionist and anti-Zionist parties had developed swiftly, even in our town.

Our Zionist group, Bnei Zion, was determined to keep Alter Yosselevitz, the Hebrew teacher, in

Steibtz. For our part, we children, organized in Zion u-Sfata, tried to find pupils for him from among the most gifted of the young children. Alter's activities were many. He established a Bnot Zion group for the women and girls; he lectured to them; on Friday nights he read aloud literary selections from *Der Jud*. On Saturday afternoons, before nightfall, he conducted Bible lessons in a *Bet Midrash* where the town rabbi's influence was not overpowering. Here before an audience of laymen and Talmud students, intelligent, "modern" members of the community selected by Alter expounded the Prophets' great chapters of Consolation and the descriptions of the Destruction in Lamentations. Their analysis followed the rules of Hebrew grammar and the spirit of the time—and the youth of the town were delighted.

The rabbi's faithful "Cossacks" were quick to declare war on Alter and his gatherings. The Great Synagogue was full of scorn for the commentators, and of muttered complaints about the heresies they preached in those Bible lessons. Everything had to be done to keep the young people of the synagogue from attending them.

The rabbi's troops suddenly acquired allies in their struggle against Alter. Among the laborers and apprentices, rumors began to spread that Alter's courses weakened and confused "class consciousness" and, instead, disseminated the poison of "chauvinistic clericalism." The charges were all rather vague at the beginning—even to the accusers themselves—but the developments were quick and surprising. One long winter night when Alter left the house of his friend Marshak, the Zionist druggist, to return to his lonely room at the edge of the town, he was suddenly attacked from behind by two peasants. One threw a sack over his head and the other began to beat him with a heavy stick. Alter somehow found the breath to ask: *"Za shtu?"* (What's this for?) The brief answer told the story: *"Za Tanach!"* (On account of the Bible.)

For a long time we tried to get to the bottom of the affair and discover which of our antagonists had organized the attack on our dear teacher: the zealots who met in the rabbi's house, or the Bundists, who were then taking their first measured, secret steps in the town, and who revealed themselves to the public eye for the first time in this Alter "affair."

It is noteworthy that the Bundists were not Steibtz' first socialists. There had been others before them, like the tutor in the household of the man who owned the tar furnaces in the nearby wood. In his early youth he had been a vastly learned yeshiva student and fervent Slonim *Hasid,* who used to sing with infinite longing Reb Aharon of Karlin's hymn, "Lord I yearn for Sabbath's loveliness" (*Yah, achsif noam Shabbat*). He was now an equally ardent unbeliever, singing with equal intensity the revolutionary chant:

Ich breng wafen
Far dem schlafen
Um zu befreien arbeits-shklafen
Un ich mach sei frei . . . *

When he cried out the word *frei*, sparks seemed to fly in the air around him and he himself seemed aflame.

However, he defined himself as an anarchist and attached no importance to the organization of the apprentices of our artisans. He was forced to leave Russia for America before his influence went very far among the "enlightened" of the town.

Michael Ruben, son of one of our prosperous families, was another pioneer radical. When he came home after his army service, he spoke polished Russian and sported a bristly mustache. He bore a striking resemblance to Gorki, and the young ladies who took care of the Russian library clustered around him. As a social revolutionary he was not concerned with Jewish workers but sought out the railway laborers, a strike in that sector then being imminent. It did not take long for Michael to be arrested.

The impact of the socialist activity going on among the Jewish proletariat in neighboring towns had not yet reached us, and our young workers— apprentices to tailors and shoemakers, tinsmiths and

* I bring weapons
  For the weak
  To liberate work-slaves
  And to make them free

carpenters and riverbank laborers, as well as seam-stresses and corset and *sheitel*-makers—felt the need for a leader.

It was then that Binyamin Leib returned home from the yeshiva in Mir.

Had he left of his own free will? Or had he been expelled for holding heretical opinions? Whatever the cause, it was clear that there had been a great change in him. He was no longer to be found studying in a synagogue; he wore the black tunic of the radical. It was known that the police had their eye on him.

That same summer Boris, son of the wealthy Iviansky family, came home from the capital city of the province where he was a student in the highest class of the commercial high school. He had, people said, been active in a students' strike there. He considered himself a "general" social democrat, but under the influence of his cousin, Boris Klatzkin (who later became a famous Yiddish publisher), he allowed himself to preach the social democratic doctrine in Yiddish to Jewish workers, without of course including any of the "exaggerated Jewish" elements characteristic of Jewish nationalism against which every good socialist was morally obligated to fight.

With the rising tide of Zionism in the town, counter-activity by the Bund began. A noted Bundist lecturer from the provincial capital was sent to

Steibtz to arrange for a public debate one Saturday between himself and Alter in the women's gallery of the New Synagogue. After the arguments were concluded, the lecturer charged Binyamin Leib, son of Isser the water bearer, and Boris Iviansky, son of the timber merchant, with joint responsibility for organizing a Bundist group in the town. They were joined by the girls of the Russian library, the apprentices and the young artisans. Thus the Steibtz branch of the Bund came into being.

From then on Binyamin Leib no longer lived in his father's house. He rented a room at the other end of the town, and all his comings and goings were shrouded in a thick veil of secrecy.

Steibtz was now to be altered almost beyond recognition.

A wave of strikes started that year: against Chayke the dressmaker and Yoshke the carpenter, against "The Odessa Shoemaker" and Gershon the tinsmith. Three apprentices went on strike here, four seamstresses there. Before one strike finished, another had begun. No one was quite sure who had lit the flame, but the fire was obviously spreading, and there was widespread suspicion that Binyamin Leib was deeply involved.

The same mysterious authority began to intervene in other disputes—between rival contractors or shopkeepers, heirs quarrelling over a legacy, husbands and wives at odds with each other. When the so-called Chevra Yosher (Association for Justice) reached a decision, it was absolutely final and there was no appeal. Rumor had it that some one who demurred was visited at night and so badly mauled that his survival was no less than a miracle.

The fear of Chevra Yosher fell upon the whole town.

There were even householders who turned to Isser the water bearer in the hope that he might be moved to intervene on their behalf with Binyamin Leib. Isser was gratified by those appeals, but refused to help anyone and roundly denied Binyamin Leib's complicity.

Night after night young people crowded the "Bundist Exchange," as Steibtz now called the Priest's Lane near the white church up on the hill. Workers on strike came and workers getting ready to strike; veterans agitating for the cause and novices eager to hear their "agitation"; the yeshiva student preparing to be a druggist's clerk and the wealthy girls studying for examinations with an externe as their tutor. The woman dentist who wanted to settle in the town was there too, and the girl normal school student from Bobroisk who spent the summer tutoring in a Steibtz household, and the town butcher's pretty daughters who sang the lyrics of Edelstein and Raisin and were always surrounded by a flock of admirers.

In the darkness of the lane behind the church, a cap glittered, and a belt buckle on a tunic shone.

The first belonged to Boris, son of the timber merchant, and the second to Binyamin Leib. For those two directed that hive of youthful activity.

That same summer—whether as visitor or fugitive—a friend of my sisters stayed for weeks at our summer house. A wandering student who had come from the Russian student colonies in Switzerland and France, he was actually one of the clandestine leaders of the Bund. Solomon, as he called himself, had a good singing voice and pleasant manners. He was thin and blue-eyed, with a blond mustache, and he brought to our house the precious gift of Yiddish songs no one in Steibtz had ever heard. Every evening his warm, fine voice could be heard singing in the woods and he captured the hearts of the young men and girls who on one pretext or another made their way to him from Steibtz and the nearby towns. Between one song and the next he raged against the *"petit bourgeois* socialists," i. e., the Poale Zion movement which was then discreetly beginning to cast its nets among the youth of the area and to which I was committed with all my heart.

One day, when it was long past lunchtime, and Solomon had not come back from his morning walk, and my sisters, too, were late, my worried mother sent me out into the wood to look for them. Since they were not to be found on any of the wider paths, I turned off to the shady alley where my sisters often sat under the nut trees and evergreens with their friends. In the distance I heard Solomon's resonant voice, coming, it seemed, from beyond the hill. I walked in that direction and found myself inside a thicket where a meeting was going on. Leaning against a tree, Solomon was addressing a large number of young people, some of them, like my sisters, summering in the wood and others from the neighboring towns. The chairman of the meeting sat on a tree stump near Solomon: it was my friend and opponent, Binyamin Leib.

I was never again to come face to face with Binyamin Leib. That year the political differences between us seemed to become as insurmountable as a high mountain; indeed, all the youth of the town were divided into two camps with that mountain between them. The sting appeared to have been taken out of the controversy between Koidenhove and Habad *Hasidim,* and certainly out of the older rift between *Hasidim* and *Mitnagdim.* Even the very recent dissension that had flared up between the Zionists and the followers of the rabbi was overshadowed. The passionate partisanship in the town now found its expression in the brand new conflict between the two clandestine "exchanges" which had sprung up almost overnight: the Bund's in the Priest's Alley, presided over by Binyamin Leib, and the even newer gathering place of the first Poale Zion on nearby Minsk Street, presided over by my friend Pinya, son of Slava-Yoshke-Barka-Henis the famous bagel baker of the town.

Pinya was two years older than I and two years younger than Binyamin Leib. Since he worked in his father's bakery, he was considered a genuine proletarian, and had many contacts with the apprentices and the thoughtful young laborers. On the other hand, he had studied Hebrew with Alter, and his uncle (his father's brother) was Rabbi Kokosh of Cherikov, one of the first of the religious Zionists to be organized in the Mizrachi movement. The rabbi's visits to our town always left a deep impression, for his sermons were both wise and witty.

Finding his supporters among the young workers who knew Hebrew and had not yet been lured by the Bund, Pinya set up a secret Poale Zion committee. The Minsk faction provided him with literature to help him organize the group, and every once in a while he brought a speaker from Minsk or Koidenhove to engage in public debate with the Bund. From then on the battle for the soul of our youth was waged furiously, with Binyamin Leib in command of one conspiratorial general staff and Pinya of the other. And I was with Pinya.

Evening after evening Pinya brought more young men and girls to our "exchange," and with the increase in numbers and activity, I, too, was drawn into political agitation.

Shoafot Ziona—the girls' Zionist group which

Alter had organized and put in my charge—gradually became the reserve corps of the Poale Zion branch. A secret mailbox was put up in the home of Sheinke Shapira, the pleasant and conscientious young chairman of the group. It was arranged that the members, when they were troubled by any ideological question, would write it down and put it into the box. Every Friday Sheinke opened the box and collected the questions which were generally written on little squares of paper which had been torn out of arithmetic notebooks. She would bring them to me, and after reading and classifying them, I would prepare detailed replies to give during my Friday night lecture to the girls.

Whenever we came upon a question full of high-sounding foreign words and subtle anti-Zionist theorizing, Sheinke would comment: "Here's another one who's listened to Binyamin Leib's speeches!"

Those were the questions I answered with particular care and emphasis, for I knew that what I said would reach beyond the poser of the question to its hidden inspirer—my chief antagonist, Binyamin Leib.

At that time Poale Zion published an anonymous Russian brochure dealing with the Bund's entrance into the Russian Social Democratic Party, and attacking the Bund's failure to recognize the special nature of the Jewish problem in the Diaspora. It was one of my duties to read sections of this brochure to the girls of Shoafot Ziona on Friday nights. The subject demanded so much study and threshing out that there were, as we knew, differences of opinion on it within the local branch of the Bund itself. The so-called "soft" faction opposed any stress on Jewish nationalism during discussions with the social democrats, while the "hard" faction insisted on emphasizing Jewish group identity. It was known that Boris and the girl teacher from Bobroisk were the leading advocates of the soft approach, and Binyamin Leib of the hard.

Pinya played with the hope that we would profit from the division within the Bund. But it did not take long for the "soft" faction to gain the upper hand and for Binyamin Leib to accept defeat. "To keep the Bund from splitting," Binyamin Leib asserted, "is more important than anything else!" And precisely because his traditional Jewish education made him suspect and because, too, he doubtless hoped to be able to influence his comrades against excessive assimilation, he took great pains to appear completely free of "nationalistic chauvinism." He raged and ranted against Zionism and Poale Zionism, both of them so hateful to him, and the atmosphere was full of hostility.

Just about then some revolutionary happening took place somewhere in Czarist Russia. Whether the governor of a province had been assassinated, or political prisoners mistreated with particular cruelty in some jail, I cannot remember, but whatever it was, the Bund in Steibtz felt impelled to act. It issued a proclamation whose Yiddish phrases were highly political. Phrases like "capitalist vampire," "lawless militarism" and "approaching judgment day" were all obviously in Binyamin Leib's style. I sensed his authorship even more clearly when my eyes were assailed by the repetition of the word *"nieder"* (down with) at the end of the proclamation. Down with bourgeois nationalism; down with *petit bourgeois* socialism; down with chauvinistic clericalism; down with Zionism.

Each *"nieder"* seemed to beat upon our heads just as once the repeated "Cursed shall you be" and "The Lord will strike you," chanted by Reb Eliahu, father of my friend, had come down like blows on the head of Isser the water bearer, father of my adversary Binyamin Leib. . . .

No counter-proclamation was issued by us till the first of May. Shortly before then, Pinya (who had gone over to the Poale Zion faction favoring political action in Russia) decided that a proclamation should be published in the name of our Poale Zion group, to serve as a reply to the Bund proclamation and at the same time to give the theoretical basis for our new program of socialism, revolution, and Zionism.

It was late at night when Pinya took me out of the town on to the road going up to the Siniava wood.

Two people were waiting for me among the trees—Elyakim the barber, who was our treasurer, and Liza Harkavy, a bright and charming gymnasia student who had come from Slutzk that spring and was the most ideologically conscious girl in the group. She was to operate the new hectograph Pinya had just brought from Minsk for the express purpose of copying our proclamation. Elyakim held the light for her to work by: it was the large lantern that Slava, Pinya's mother, used every night to bring all the bagels and cakes she had baked to market. By the light of that lantern Liza incised the words I dictated on the new waxed sheet. This was my first proclamation.

How my heart beat on that first of May when I passed the synagogue courtyard and saw a group of excited young people crowding near the wall, eagerly reading over each other's shoulders the illegal words that were so full of fire.

I had to muster all my self-control to keep my face from revealing whose words they were.

The one person whose image had haunted my mind all the time I was writing the proclamation was never to read it. Two days before the first of May smallpox broke out in the town, claiming Binyamin Leib as one of its first victims. All Dr. Levitan's efforts to save him were to no avail. Within a week Binyamin Leib was dead.

The conspiratorial atmosphere that had enveloped the Bund suddenly vanished. All its members, supporters, and sympathizers, grief-stricken and stunned, made their way to the secret lodgings of the young leader who had been so cruelly cut off. The funeral turned into a demonstration. For the first time in our town's history the streets saw the dead body of a Jew wrapped not in a prayer shawl but in a red flag. The body was followed not by the sextons of the Burial Society with alms boxes in their hands, and not by Talmud Torah children with verses of the Psalms on their lips, but by bare-headed young men and long-haired young women marching together, carrying red flags and singing revolutionary songs. Suddenly the beautiful Devora, daughter of Leizer the butcher, stepped forward and began to sing in a tearful voice:

> *Es treft dir a koil, mein getreier,*
> *A koil fun'm sayneh, dem hund,*
> *Ich nem dir arois fun'm feier*
> *Un heil dir mit kushen dein wund . . .* *

One mourner stood apart in all the marching, singing procession of young people. Isser the water bearer seemed a stranger at this funeral, which was less a funeral than a demonstration. Could it really

---

* A bullet has wounded you, beloved,
A bullet shot by the enemy, that dog.
I take you away from the firing line
And heal you by kissing your wound . . .

be his son, his Binyamin Leib—his firstborn and his final hope—who was being brought to eternal rest?

The pain of his bereavement was sharpened by the indignity of his loneliness, a loneliness more acute than he had ever experienced in all his sorrowful years. He had lived to see the realization of his greatest hope—the mark of degradation was completely removed from his oldest son. Indeed, the finest young people in the town had come together to pay honor to his Binyamin Leib. But, Lord of the Universe, why did they do it in such a strange way? Why was there not even one Jew of his own kind at the funeral of his son? Why did they refuse to let him, the father, say *Kaddish*, and why had they all forgotten that *El Male Rahamim* should be recited?

When the procession reached the courtyard of the synagogue and went on as if there were no synagogue there at all, or as if there had never been any relationship between that building and the dead youth, Isser's agony became unbearable. His feet would carry him no further. Silently, he slipped out of the ranks of the alien funeral procession and with his last breath staggered into the empty synagogue. In his habitual posture he rested his elbows on the window sill in the western wall—and burst into tears.

This was the first time in a life of endless grief and self-control that Isser the water bearer was seen crying out loud, within the synagogue itself. . . .

My First
Conference

It was a regional conference, the first such of Poale Zion in Lithuania and White Russia. It convened in absolute secrecy in Minsk during June, 1906.

This was my first year as a member of the Party —and I had had to keep my new affiliation secret not only from the police but even from the girls' Zionist Society, Shoafot Ziona, which our town Hebrew teacher, Alter Yosselevitz had established as a youth auxiliary to the Women's Zionist movement,

Bnot Zion, founded and led by him; he had chosen me to "lead" the younger group.

The head of our General Zionist association, Mordecai Marshak, owner of the pharmacy, had also secretly entered Poale Zion when a group was clandestinely set up in Steibtz by emissaries from Minsk.

The organization of self-defense in the town was our young Party's first activity, and when in the New Synagogue after Evening Prayers one day we appealed to the youth to join, and to the adults to contribute money for equipment, it was I—all of fifteen years of age and only one month in the Party —who was asked to make the public speech. This was my first political address to a public gathering, and my fright before I delivered it has remained with me through the years. Pinya Kushnir, whose mother was our famous bagel baker, was the organizer. He mounted the platform, struck the table, and warned that no one was to dare to leave the synagogue before I finished. The door was barred and "guards" stood by. When I was through, Pinya announced the contributions. A week later he and I were sent by the Party's regional headquarters in Minsk to organize self-defense units in the nearby small towns of Svirzna, Baranovitz, Mush, Lechavitz, and Gorodzia. In each case we turned first to our Poale Zion comrades and with their help saw to it that the general meeting, as well as the self-defense organization itself, should be non-partisan. Wherever possible, a Bundist or General Zionist leader spoke along with us, and even though fear of the police kept some householders from coming to the assembly in the synagogue, many of them, when visited at home, responded to the appeal.

Returning to Steibtz after this first "campaign," we found the town terror-struck by rumors of impending attack. We decided upon a meeting in the Old Synagogue on the Great Sabbath (before Passover), immediately after the rabbi's sermon. Pinya was of course chairman; and the leader of the Bund, my schoolmate and dear rival, Hirschel Neifeld, addressed the group after I was done speaking. When the two of us had finished, my uncle, Joel Ginsburg, one of our respected and wealthier citizens, made his way to the platform, and instead of upbraiding us—as I feared—for violating the sanctity of so holy a Sabbath, called out: "The right is on the side of these boys, and it is our duty to help them, for the danger is upon us." And that Saturday night contributions of money were brought to my uncle's house, enabling Pinya to go to Minsk the next morning and purchase revolvers. Our self-defense unit soon numbered a hundred trained and equipped members divided into groups of ten. Its turn to act soon came.

Word spread that an attack was to take place on Sunday after church. We knew that instigators had come from distant places; we saw peasant women arriving with empty wagons, which, it was understood, they expected to fill with the booty robbed from the Jews. From early in the morning our members were stationed in the market place, lead-tipped iron bars in their hands and lead-tipped leather thongs in their pockets. The heads of our groups carried concealed revolvers and divided the watch over the market place among themselves.

At noon an agitated and incited crowd, all ready for the attack, came pouring out of the white church above the market place. One of the "guests" rushed to the fore, dragging the peasants after him towards the stores. At that moment all the revolvers, scattered over the market place, went off at once. They shot into the air and hurt no one, but even that was enough to intimidate the crowd. Bedlam ensued. The horses were frightened, the peasant women screamed as if they were being slaughtered, and the wagons collided with each other. The peasants ran with their last breath, fleeing from the armed Jews. And the revolvers kept on shooting. In a few moments the market place was empty. . . .

In this very first year of its existence Poale Zion was affected by a two-fold split: not only was there a division between Territorialists and "Palestinians" in the movement, but within each camp some advocated and others opposed participation in Russian revolutionary activity. Zar, the teacher and theoretician, had been our town's delegate to the Poale Zion conference held in Minsk under the leadership of Rubenchik early in 1905. There he led the fight for Zion and for the revolution (they called us Palestintzes–Politische Kempfer). That year on the first of May we distributed throughout Steibtz a stencilled proclamation in defense of our approach. This was the first May Day Proclamation I had ever written.

With youthful enthusiasm and considerable linguistic struggle, I began to do translating, too, turning from Russian into Yiddish Ber Borochov's series of theoretical articles called *"Nasha Platforma"* ("Our Platform"), which under the pen name of Postoyani appeared at long intervals in the journal *Yevreiskaya Rabotchaya Chronica* that Poale Zion had started in Poltava. I sent my translations to the newly established Central Committee of Poale Zion social democrats in Lodz, which was then attempting, through its emissaries, to gather around it all those in the badly split movement who had remained faithful to Zion and not gone astray after the Territorialists or been infected by the apolitical approach of the Minsk group or the optimism of the Siamists. The first regional conference of our group, the new Poale Zion social democrats, was then being called together to meet in Minsk. To my utter astonishment it was suggested that I be the delegate from Steibtz.

I remember my trepidation very clearly, and

how unfit I felt for the responsibility being thrust on me. With the naiveté of the young I was certain that the fate of the Jewish people depended upon the deliberations of this secret meeting and, therefore, only persons of the most exceptional ability should take part in it.

True, our theoretician, Zar, had left the town, but there was Marshak, who was the oldest among us and the most balanced in judgment. He ought to represent us and set forth our point of view, I thought. But it was Marshak himself who had proposed my name and defended the suggestion heatedly. Once the voting was over and I was elected, there was no turning back. I could only utter a silent prayer in my heart: "Lord of the world, may I bring no disgrace on the conference. . . ."

There was a domestic aspect to all this—complicated but comical—which I had to manage somehow: how was I going to tell the family about a decision which had to be kept completely secret? How could I suddenly go off to Minsk for a week without giving a reason? And where could I find an adequate reason? We had taken our vote on Thursday and the conference in Minsk was to begin on Sunday. I had to be there before noon.

I arrived home on Thursday night in a state of complete perplexity, but by the next morning I had an inspiration: my eyes, I told Mother, were troubling me. They continued to trouble me all of Friday and

Saturday. I remember how distressed the household was, particularly since there was no physician in Steibtz with specialized knowledge of eye diseases. On Saturday night I overheard Father saying to Mother: "The only thing to do, Sorke, is to send the boy to Minsk tomorrow and have Dr. Kaminski examine him."

Father wrote down the doctor's address for me, gave me money for the trip and half a ruble for the doctor, and sent me off with his blessing. Aided by his kindness, I reached the conference exactly on time. . . .

It was, as I have said, a secret meeting which moved from place to place for fear of the police. I can remember four different houses where we held our sessions during the week. All four belonged to wealthy Jews who were spending their summer holidays in the country and had left trusted employees or poor relatives to look after their homes. The guardians, in each case, were members of our Party who despite the risk to themselves opened the grand halls to us.

I recall how while we were meeting in a house in the Upper Market, a message came from outside: "The police are on their way!" We put out all the lights immediately and the speaker went on talking in the dark. A large, open volume of Gemorra dimmed the light of the one candle on the little table in a corner. Bent over alongside it sat the three secretaries of the conference, writing their minutes in pencil.

There were some three dozen delegates, all of whom with the exception of two or three were very young, between sixteen and twenty years old. We were all from the regions of Vilna, Kovna, Grodna, and Minsk. There was not one girl among us.

Motel Bogin, who came from Minsk, was responsible for the organization of the conference and for the arrangements. Under a changed name he was to become one of the leaders of the Party in America. Sharing the chairmanship of the meetings with him were Moshe Lieb from Vilna, who later became a merchant and broke away from the movement, and Abraham Zeidschnur, whom I remember as already wearing a trim, little beard. He later married the most devoted girl in our Vilna group, Sarah Luria. The two were to die in the days of annihilation: he was put to death in the Ponari Camp near Vilna, and she died in exile in far-off Uzbekistan.

The delegate to the conference from the movement's carefully hidden Central Committee was Leon Berlineraut of Moscow, a rather proper young student, bespectacled and smooth shaven, who spoke impeccable Russian. He was like a well-brought up youngster who had fallen in with a wild "gang."

I was one of the three secretaries and was responsible for the Hebrew protocol. The minutes in Yiddish were the work of one of the older delegates, a teacher in an elementary school who knew an amazing number of Yiddish poems by heart. The secretary for Russian, a very astute speaker, too, was young Haikel Mogilevitch of Brogin. I was told years later that he became a member of a Zionist student "corporation" in Switzerland, and went about in one of those special caps, with colored ribbons crosswise on his chest, defending Hebrew against the Yiddishists in the colony. After that he was a *Yevsek* commissar in Saratov, persecuting Zionists mercilessly. Then all trace of him was lost.

One of the delegates I remember best was Velvel, the brother of Alexander Hashin (who was then still called Vitebsky and considered one of the brilliant minds in the Party). Velvel later turned against Zionism and was known to his allies in the Arab East as Abu-Ziame. He caused us tremendous difficulties. In the end his fate was as bitter as that of his more gifted brother whom he admired immensely through all the vicissitudes and changes of life and thought. Both perished in the cellars of the G.P.U.

From Smorgon there was a not so young Hebrew teacher who stuttered while trying to express his strong emotions and was infuriated by his inability to make himself clear to the impatient group. He settled in Israel, working, I think, in Jerusalem.

From Mir there was Shaike Tiktinsky, grandson of Reb Chaim, the famous head of the yeshiva, and son of his successor, the blind Reb Abraham. You could recognize his father's sightless eyes in his young face. He came to Israel with the Third *Aliya* and worked for years in the Immigration Department of the Jewish Agency.

From Bialistok there was "Lippe"—Lippman Sukenik, who was to be the famous professor of archeology in the Hebrew University of Jerusalem and the father of another famous archeologist, General Yigael Yadin.

Another "Lippe" arrived from Bobroisk in the middle of the conference. This was Lippman Levinson, delegate of the little Poale Zion group in his town.

There were two central dominating figures on whose presentations the discussions at the conference were based, and whose personalities and ideas influenced and indeed shaped the movement for a long period after the conference ended. The two were Ovadia, who was later called Avner—in actuality Yitzhak Ben-Zvi—and Joseph Eisenstadt, the father of the scholarly Dr. Shmuel Eisenstadt of Tel Aviv.

Ovadia was a legend and a hero for all of us. We knew that he had headed the self-defense in the south and been arrested, and we knew, too, that the devoted Abraham Machtey (who unfortunately could not manage to come to the conference) had organized a group which succeeded in freeing Ovadia. Risking their own lives, they had snatched him from under the nose of the police convoy.

Ovadia was the only member of the Central Committee who had been to *Eretz Yisrael*; he planned to return there and no one could compare with him in expert knowledge of the Land. The knowledgeable ones among us were aware that in "*Nasha Platforma*," the basic written text of our new Party, the chapters dealing with the realities of *Eretz Yisrael*, were based on his material. The word went about that a committee of three in Poltava had been selected to draw up the "platform:" Borochov, Vitebsky (that is, Hashin) and Avner (that is, Ben-Zvi). Borochov was responsible for the theoretical analysis; Hashin put his stamp on the polemical material; and Ben-Zvi dealt with "realization," that is, the chapters concerned with the carrying out of the program in *Eretz Yisrael*.

It was about "realization" that he lectured at the conference, demonstrating extraordinarily detailed knowledge of matters about which none of us had the least idea. In his analysis of the Arab problem, he demonstrated that there was no such thing as a unified Arab nation in the country. There were various ethnic groups, various religions and tribes and great families that were bitterly hostile to each other. These could not be united into a people unless we so badly mishandled the situation that they would draw together. Their alleged spokesmen, he asserted, were reactionary effendis who enslaved the population: we should not even be in touch with them. The case of the Arab workers was quite different. As soon as they were organized, we would be their allies. In fact, the economy of the country needed European laborers, for there were functions necessary to it which Arabs could not perform, while, on the other hand, certain aspects of the economy would surely continue to be monopolized by Arabs, since Europeans would not be able to adjust themselves to those types of work. This was a "natural" division of labor, and if only we knew how to arrange it there would be no competition between the two groups.

With the aid of innumerable facts, and Turkish and Arabic names unknown to us, and statistical proofs for which we were eager, Ovadia made his points and set us at ease. It became absolutely clear to us that our idea was feasible and in fact bound to become reality. . . .

Most important of all was the great confidence Ovadia inspired as soon as he appeared. He was tall and slim, with a little black beard just beginning to sprout at the edge of his chin. His eyes expressed complete honesty, and the way he dressed bore witness to an austere way of life. One realized with the first glance at that elongated, pure face that the legends about his zeal and dedication were true to fact. Though I knew he was a student at the University of Kiev—his Russian style was proof of that—I could not help but see him as a sort of emissary from the Holy Land, a modern version of those emissaries who came to our home year in and year out from Safad or Tiberias. One evening we persuaded him to sing some of the songs from *Eretz Yisrael,* and when in his deep bass he sang the then very popular *"Atzei Shittim Omdim"* ("Acacia Trees Are Standing"), he himself seemed to resemble a marvellous tall tree standing on watch from ancient times. . . .

If Ovadia represented the dominant group in the movement, Joseph Eisenstadt was the opposition. There were legends about him, too. He had been arrested in Poltava with Borochov, and the news of his release had appeared in *Chronica* very shortly before the conference assembled. He was a banker and prosperous business man in Borisov; a friend and ideological opponent of his, my Bundist acquaintance from Borisov, was later to tell me that if two financial propositions were made to Banker Eisenstadt, one requiring little work on his part and sure to bring him considerable profit and the other needing long and complicated treatment while the profit was problematical, Eisenstadt would surely choose the second because it was "more interesting." In addition, I knew what my Bundist acquaintance did not: that Eisenstadt had given his learned friend, Reb Samuel Alexandrov of Bobroisk, the money he needed to publish his *Pach ha-Shemen* and *Masechet Negaim,* for one of which Eisenstadt even wrote an introduction. And then there was Eisenstadt's humor: though he was the oldest delegate at the conference, he was the gayest and wittiest of them all, invariably the life of the meeting.

I remember how he rushed into the room one day with a very sad expression on his face. "Comrades, give me your sympathy! I've had a terrible railway accident!"

Frightened, all of us asked; "What is it? What actually happened, Haver Eisenstadt?"

"My wife has just arrived on the train," he answered.

His political statement bore all the marks of his lively temperament. Sprinkled with folk-sayings and scholarly adages, it was intended to prove that there was a vast difference between our struggle in Russia and our struggle in *Eretz Yisrael.* In Russia we should fight the Bund to the bitter end, for the downfall of the Czar would be no help to us and working toward it would simply waste our time. On the other hand, in *Eretz Yisrael* we had to be the Bund—no less than that but also no more. There we should work toward strictly limited objectives: the downfall of the Sultan and the democratization of Turkey; the rest would come by itself and there was no need for a program. Democratization would lead to immigration; immigration to colonization; colonization to realization of a territorial center—

and thus our goal would be attained. In order to overthrow the Sultan we should join forces with the Young Turks and young Arabs and whoever else could help to change the regime in Turkey.

It was on Thursday evening that Eisenstadt gave his lecture. It proved so provocative that every one rushed to enter his name on the list of those wishing to participate in the debate. Just then our "monitors" came in to announce that there was suspicious activity outside. The session stopped abruptly. It was not resumed the next day, and the debate on Joseph Eisenstadt's statement, which promised to be so lively and stormy, never took place. In fact, the conference was not concluded.

On the Thursday morning before Eisenstadt's speech, Abraham Zeidschnur, our organizer, had wisely suggested that the delegates elect a regional committee without waiting for the final session, since no one could know if or how the conference would end. And on Friday morning I was told at my lodgings that the committee, which had indeed been elected the day before, was meeting at Reb Meir Halprin's Hebrew Book Store and I was to appear before it to be told what would be required of me.

Though I had only been active in the Party for little more than a year, a number of recent experiences had so profoundly affected me that I was ready to accept any duties the Party would impose upon me. After returning from my "campaign" to organize self-defense units in the small towns of the neighborhood, I had determined not to remain in Steibtz, but, having completed my Talmud studies, to go where I could learn general subjects under the guidance of a good teacher. We had no such tutor in the town, and Father, understanding my concern, sent me to live with my uncle in Baranowitz. This was my mother's brother of whom all our household was very fond and who was a fervent Zionist. With a non-Jewish student in Baranowitz, I began to study Russian and all the other subjects which appeared on the special examinations set for externe students.

I have a vivid memory of the railway strike which took place at that time. I recall going to the railroad station with my aunt and uncle to find out when our connection with the outside world would be resumed. And I recall my constant arguments with the Territorialists, who were particularly strong in the town. There was even a secret meeting of the Territorialists in the library one night where, standing up to speak, I suddenly noticed to my consternation that my uncle was in the audience. I had never imagined that he would come at night to an illegal meeting of that kind, and he, for his part, could not believe that it was really I who was addressing the public.

It did not take long till the police discovered that my teacher was a socialist revolutionary work-

ing among the railway laborers. He was imprisoned
—and I remained without a teacher.

Then Father sent me to stay with his older
brother in Dubrovna, Father's birthplace. This uncle,
together with his aged father-in-law, owned a well-
known, long-established factory for prayer shawls.
Its "salesmen" travelled to all Jewish communities
within the Pale of Settlement to sell wide woolen
shawls as well as silk shawls woven in the factory
owned by my uncle's son. Their factories were on
one side of the Dnieper, the so-called "small side,"
while on the "large side" a big modern weaving
factory had been established by ICA, the Jewish
Colonization Association. I used to wander about
among the weavers' houses, and it was there for the
first time that I met Jewish poverty in all its ghast-
liness. My heart ached at the sight of the wretched
homes of the "private" weavers who wove *talesim*
on their own looms and brought them to the factory
to sell. Pious Jews with large families to care for,
these workers labored from dawn to dark, and never
had enough food in the house; they, their wives and
their pale, sickly children were literally on the verge
of starvation. I could not concentrate on the subjects
I was being taught by a new student-tutor, hailing,
as it happened, from the town of Orsha. In a few
weeks' time I was a member of the town Poale Zion
committee and undertook to organize a weavers'
strike against my uncle—my host whom I truly

loved. When the strike broke out and my part in it was discovered, I had no alternative but to leave my uncle's home and town.

I remember how when I returned to Steibtz I met with my comrades in the woods and described what I had learned about the dreadful poverty of those genuine Jewish workers—genuine both as Jews and as members of the proletariat. I knew that despite all my craving for scholarship, I would be unable to go on studying unless I could at the same time serve the Jewish labor movement in whatever manner was required of me. It was then that the covenant between Poale Zion and myself was sealed.

So as I walked in Minsk that morning to Meir Halprin's bookstore (the Meir Halprin who wrote *Sefer ha-Notrikon* and whose son-in-law, Michal Rabinowitz, was to be the famous Jerusalem scholar and bookshop owner), I knew that I would agree to the regional committee's request without doubt or question. But in my heart I vowed that though I would dedicate myself to the work of the movement, I would always find time for systematic study.

Entering the bookstore, I found the members of the committee hidden in a tiny room in back of the counter. Motel Bogin and Abraham Zeidschnur came out to tell me that it had been decided that the movement would establish its own publishing house under the name of The Hammer, and would also issue a bi-weekly periodical in Vilna. I would have to be ready to move there whenever the summons came, for the leaders of the Party wrote in Russian and since the paper had to be in Yiddish, I was needed as translator.

At that moment I had absolutely no idea how I would tell the family about the decision or how I would manage to get their consent or how, for that matter, I would continue to study while carrying out the duties the Party imposed on me. But that I would carry them out, I was sure—and I did.

It was Friday morning when the interview in the bookstore took place, and after it was over I started to walk directly to the train station so that I might get home before the Sabbath began.

On the way the thought struck me suddenly that the whole week had passed without my going to the eye doctor whose address Father had written down for me; the half-ruble Father had given me for the doctor's fee was still in my purse. I turned off at once to the nearby street where Dr. Kaminski lived. He examined my eyes and, to my surprise, prescribed glasses.

I have been wearing glasses ever since.

Baron Ginzburg's
"Academy"

☆

For Russian Jewry at the beginning of this century, *Wissenschaft des Judentums,* the scientific study of Jewish subjects, was still an exotic Western growth. Those who were eager for modern Jewish scholarship made their way to the West or absorbed the work of Galician or German academicians at second hand from translations that appeared in Russian Jewish monthlies or from Hebrew versions by such distinguished writers as A. E. Harkavy and S. P. Rabinowitz. Among Russian Jews there were only very few who were open to the West and interested in grafting Western scientific method upon the profound traditional learning of Eastern Jewry.

One of the most distinguished members of this little group was Baron David Ginzburg, youngest scion of the house of Jewish aristocrats who for three generations, from the time of the Napoleonic War to the beginnings of parliamentary democracy in the Czarist Empire, had been Russia's leading Jewish family. For years the scholarly Baron dreamed of establishing an institute of Jewish studies in the capital city of Russia. Yet, despite his special connections with prominent figures in the Government, he could not get a permit to establish his institute until he began to describe it by the non-committal name of "an advanced school of Oriental Studies," and further agreed that it would not enjoy academic standing and that studying at the school would not give the students the right to live in St. Petersburg. Nor did the Baron receive financial help from any public fund or institution, not even from the Disseminators of Enlightenment (*Mefitzei Haskala beYisrael*), which association he himself headed, nor from the Jewish Colonization Association of which he was one of the directors. Actually, the institute, which was popularly known as "The Academy of Jewish Studies," came into being with no help of any sort from any political or communal body and was entirely dependent upon the Baron's devotion and good name.

When I came to the Academy in the fall of 1907, I found six or seven students who had preceded me, all of them from provincial towns, all of them fervently eager to study, almost all of them without means, and most of them without permits to reside in St. Petersburg, which was of course outside the Pale of Jewish Settlement. Among them were former students of the traditional *Bet Midrash* and some who were already leaders of Zionist and revolutionary movements.

The Academy still had no building of its own, and all the lectures were given in Baron Ginzburg's private library. Students were accepted after passing a unique type of examination: the Baron would engage each applicant in a long and detailed conversation about a number of Jewish and general topics, some scholarly, others of public and communal interest. Those who were admitted to the Academy but had no residence permit were turned over to the care of the Baron's steward, Piotr Alexeievitz: he found lodgings for them and assigned them to occupations whose practitioners were entitled to live in the city. That is to say, by means of regular payments to various artisans and to the police inspectors in their districts, students were registered as painters or ink-makers, or waiters and doorkeepers in wealthy

Jewish homes. Lest a police inspector who had not yet been bribed come to look for them, they had to appear at fixed hours in their "places of employment."

The official opening of the Academy took place in January, 1908, in the presence of a large audience which included the leading Jewish writers, scholars, and cultured laymen of the capital. A building had been purchased adjoining the Baron's private residence. On the top floor a kosher restaurant was opened, which served all the Jewish students in the city and was managed chiefly by the students themselves. The house became a magnet and drew to itself Jewish academic youth of every sort of ideological persuasion. During 1908 a group from the University of St. Petersburg entered the Academy, and a year later they were joined by a number of graduates of the modern yeshiva established in Odessa by Bialik, Klausner, and Rav Tzair (Chernowitz).

For the opening of the Academy, a full program of studies was prepared and printed. The list of the faculty included some very famous names, as well as the names of young scholars whose only recommendation was the confidence the Baron had in them. He had turned to promising new people because he had met with great difficulty in assembling his faculty. He had had to reconcile himself, for instance, to doing without the two greatest Jewish scholars in

Russia. One was the aged Professor Daniel Chwolson, the famous Orientalist, from whose teaching, the Baron felt, the Academy's students would have benefited immeasurably. Chwolson had courageously defended Jews and Judaism against the blood libels recurrently hurled at them; he had warmly encouraged the Baron to establish the Academy "lest Torah be forgotten in Israel." But the Baron, who admired his scholarship immensely, could not possibly ask him—nor, in point of fact, did he wish to ask him—to join the teaching staff. For Chwolson had been converted to Christianity decades back and had trained two generations of Russian Orthodox priests. Though even famous rabbis were rather lenient in their attitude toward him, the Baron could never forgive any convert. For all that, he was later to arrange to have the students go to Chwolson's home for lectures on Hebrew grammar. It was the last winter of Chwolson's life—he was more than ninety years old and had to be carried into the room in a rocking chair. Wrapped in woolen blankets, he never moved out of the chair, and the voice that spoke to us in Russian with a strong Jewish accent was the voice of a dying man.

The case of the second great scholar was altogether different. This was the head of the Oriental Department of the Royal Library, old Abraham Eliahu Harkavy, of whom the Baron spoke with all the admiration of a student for a master. Harkavy was of great assistance to the Baron in planning the Academy, but he absolutely refused to teach in it. He felt bound by the vow he had made to Rabbi Isaac Elhanan, one of the most venerated rabbis of Russia: he had solemnly promised that he would never teach in a modern rabbincal seminary should an institution of that Western European type ever be established in Russia. The rabbis knew that without Harkavy's participation no such seminary would be possible, and they insisted on his taking the vow, since otherwise he might be influenced by the *Mefitzei Haskala,* who were in fact responsible for his appointment to the Library and his retention of the post. Harkavy was so faithful to his pledge and so fearful of any possible involvement that he could not be convinced even by the Baron, his friend and collaborator in *The Jewish Encyclopedia.* In vain did the Baron point out that the Academy had not been established in order to train rabbis and was concerned only with the advancement of pure scholarship, untouched by professional considerations. In vain, too, did the students tell Harkavy of their utter disinclination to become Government-appointed rabbis.

The Baron had gotten Dr. J. L. Katznelson, editor of *The Jewish Encyclopedia,* to teach the history of *halakhah.* Under the pseudonym of Buki Ben Yagli, Dr. Katznelson wrote Hebrew stories which we knew and loved. His lectures on the Talmud

quickly became very popular, for he had much to of-
fer even to those of us who were steeped in Gemorra.
He would analyze disputed issues by referring to
the social and religious conditions among the Jews
of Babylon or Palestine and among the neighboring
peoples. Very often he would stray into the side-
paths that were so dear to him as a physician and
discuss medicine in the Talmud, the laws of purity
in the Bible and in later tradition, and the influence
of Zoroastrianism on talmudic legislation, all of these
subjects of life-long study on his part.

History was taught us by the most famous
historian in Russian Jewry, Shimon Dubnow. Over
the three years of our course his lectures covered the
whole of Jewish history, from its biblical beginnings
to our day. Master architect in historiography, he
built his lectures with utmost care, assigning to each
period its proportionate place in the entire structure.
He was then completing his great ten-volume history, perfecting its structure and checking the ac-
curacy of all the details. The chapters, as prepared,
served as the basis of his lectures, and he was at the
same time publishing his introductory summaries in
the historical quarterly he edited. During the first
year he devoted a good deal of attention to the
development of historiography, the classification of
periods, and the sociological method which he ap-
plied in his studies. Though the particular field to
which he had made distinguished and novel con-

tributions was modern Jewish history in Eastern Europe, he gave his preliminary lectures on the biblical period so effectively that what he said about modern biblical criticism opened new worlds to us. And the lessons in which he worked on modern source materials gave us our first training in independent research.

Dubnow's lectures, always given on Thursday and Saturday evenings, were held in a truly festive atmosphere. The large hall of the Academy was full of young men and women, many of them students from the University and the Polytechnion or the women's university in St. Petersburg. Dubnow lectured from a sitting position; his voice was strong and clear, his Russian style rich and picturesque. Though he dealt with innumerable details in each of his two hour lectures, one always felt his deep sense of reverence for the destiny of our unique people and for the organic unity he wove out of all those varied and distinct facts.

I recall a significant instance of the special reverence young people felt for Dubnow's lectures. One of those who came to listen to him on Thursday evenings was Joseph Trumpeldor, the tall, vigorous, one-armed hero of Port Arthur. He was a famous figure in Russian Jewry, and we Labor Zionists knew that he dreamed of establishing a completely independent and vocationally self-sustaining *kvutza* or commune in Palestine, an idea the merits of which we frequently debated. One Thursday, a little before Dubnow's lecture was scheduled to begin, Trumpeldor suddenly appeared in my room. He was dressed in his bemedalled officer's uniform, which he had had to wear that day since it was an official holiday. "I've come to change my clothes," he said. "This foreign uniform would desecrate the hall in which our great historican lectures on the past of our people."

The younger scholars on the faculty were clearly beginning to believe that it would no longer be possible for one man to write the entire history of the Jewish people. The time of Jost, Graetz and Dubnow, they felt, was over, and so much knowledge was required for each period and each country that future histories would have to be the collective work of a group of scholars, each discussing the period about which he had specialized knowledge. Hence scholars had best choose whatever facet of Jewish history was most interesting to them and devote themselves to it.

Dubnow was opposed to this view. What he tried to impress upon his students was a consciousness of the interrelationships and continuous development of Jewish history. For in his view, all Jewish history constituted a single human creation, each period being rooted in the one preceding it, deriving from it and at the same time generating the subsequent age. Leaving out a period was like cutting an act out of a play that had been constructed as an artistic unit. As for the specialists in particular periods, all they did, really, was to prepare the bricks for a future building. The true architect in historiography, Dubnow emphasized, was he who knew how to put the bricks together into a many-storied, well-constructed building. Only those who planned to master the intricacies of the entire building would be accepted as his disciples.

While Dubnow's public lectures were devoted to the general processes of Jewish history, his seminars were concerned with the study of minute details. A small group of students would sit in a circle around him, one or another of us serving as lecturer while our teacher listened attentively and led us in discussion. We soon became very fond of these seminar meetings. I still remember how hard I worked on my first lecture. Its subject was the *Memoirs of Gluckel of Hameln* as a source for the history of Jewish communities in seventeenth-century Europe. The Yiddish manuscript of the *Memoirs* had just been published by Professor Kaufmann, and for months I collected material from rabbinical Responsa and homiletics and community records—all serving as background for the elucidation of what that extraordinary woman had written. Years later, when I participated in the seminars of Friedrich Meinecke in Freiburg and Eduard Meier in Berlin, I realized how much I had learned about historic method from our group meetings with Dubnow.

In addition to his public lectures and private seminars, Dubnow taught us in still a third way: he had one or another of us accompany him on the stroll he took through the city every day between four and six in the afternoon. This was his recreation after working long hours at his many projects— the great *History* he was preparing for publication, the *History of Hasidism* he was writing, the historical quarterly he edited, the lectures he prepared for the Academy, and the many communal activities in which he played a leading role. As teacher and student walked together, there were always unforgettable talks.

Then there was the crucial incident before our final examinations, when we came to his study and asked him to tell us what period of Jewish history he would emphasize in his questions so that we might know on what to concentrate in our last weeks of study. He looked at us very sadly and said: "An intelligent Jew must feel completely at home in every period of Jewish history."

I was truly frightened of the burden he seemed to be imposing on us, and it was only when I was more mature that I began to understand what he meant when he spoke of the essential unity of Jewish history—a unity which he lived in himself and wanted us, his pupils, to feel as he did.

If Dubnow and Dr. Katznelson were our most famous teachers, we had younger but very gifted instructors in a number of disciplines. There was Dr. Abraham Zarzovsky in Philology, Dr. A. P. Kaminetsky in Apocrypha, Dr. Jonah J. Ginsburg in Arabic, Dr. S. M. Goldstein in Russian Jewish History. There was I. D. Markon, pupil of Chwolson and Harkavy and then of Steinschneider, who worked in the Royal Library, followed in the footsteps of Harkavy, and taught us Medieval Hebrew Literature, paying special attention to the Karaites. In the world of Talmud there were Rabbi Aryeh Karlin and the lawyer, H. B. Slossberg. The former was modest and retiring, a brilliant product of the Lithuanian yeshivot, who had studied dentistry in order not to be dependent upon a rabbinical post and, at the same time, to be able to receive permission to reside in St. Petersburg. He contributed articles on legal and historic aspects of the Talmud to *The Jewish Encyclopedia*. Slossberg, who had studied in a yeshiva during his youth, had become a famous jurist, was politically active, and was a defender of Jewish rights in Russia along with the distinguished M. M. Vinaver. Rabbi Karlin would sit at the head of the table, expounding a talmudic problem with a Gemorra and a volume of Maimonides' *Yad ha-Hazaka* open before him, while

Slossberg followed his exposition by referring to German and Russian translations of the Talmud. He would then add a legal commentary on the case from the point of view of Roman law and the modern juridical concepts accepted in the West and Russia. In his memoirs, written while he was a political émigré in Paris, he spoke with great warmth about his work at the Academy and about the Baron.

But it was actually Baron Ginzburg himself who was the greatest of our teachers. *The Jewish Encyclopedia* in Russian, which he edited, contained a small biographical item about him, in which with characteristic modesty he refused to have even his chief scholarly publications listed or his picture printed. The article did state, however, that he lectured at the Academy "on Talmudic and Rabbinic Literature, Arabic Literature, Semitic Philology, and Religious Philosophy." Actually he taught and conducted seminars in all these diciplines, each of them reinforcing and sustaining the others. He never became reconciled to the division of Jewish scholarship into clearly defined subjects. Though he agreed that the highly specialized knowledge required for each subject made special instructors necessary, the material itself seemed to him to tolerate no divisions. The true scholar, he felt, made his way through all the separate segments of Torah as though they were interrelated parts of a single mansion, and taught his students accordingly. Had time permitted and academic opinion tolerated it, he would gladly have taught every branch of Jewish scholarship. He did so during the Academy's first year when he was our only teacher and all our studying was done in the rooms of his library.

Even after the curriculum was subdivided, all the courses he taught were connected with each other and formed a single intellectual unit, the axis on which all of them revolved being Jewish thought regarding God, the world, and the Jewish people. When he read Gemorra with us, he gave particular emphasis to the mystic concept of *Merkava,* the Chariot. When he concerned himself with literary history, he devoted a whole winter term to Philo of Alexandria and the intellectual links between him and Plato. For an entire year he taught us Hasdai Crescas' *Or Adonai,* the Ralbag's *Milhamot Elohim,* and *Tagmulai ha-Nephesh* by Hillel of Verona. He lectured at length on each of them, and in our discussion groups with him we analyzed them chapter by chapter. Invariably, he would add explanations in his rich Russian slightly tinged with a French accent. As he presented them to us, the ideas in the texts were seen against the background of the entire development of world religious-philosophical thought, as well as the work of previous Jewish thinkers.

Whenever he came into a room to teach, he

brought with him a satchel full of books which were open at the relevant places or stuck full of little bits of paper that indicated the chapters and pages he intended to refer to. Never reading from a prepared text, he was always remarkably well prepared, and after the lecture he would set up his whole pile of books for us to examine. When any of us scanned them or asked for additional explanations, he was delighted beyond words.

A uniquely interesting world opened before us when he lectured on Hebrew philology. He seemed to swim through seas of lexicography, and was in fact said to be the master of thirty-six languages and of all the intricacies of their respective grammars. When he entered the classroom, he was always followed by one of his servants carrying dictionaries of various kinds which we would then see the Baron consulting like a true polyglot. He found pleasure in pointing out both what was common to various languages and what was peculiar to one or another and entirely without parallel. Classifying words by their families and by the development they had gone through during the ages, he touched upon all the languages of man and upon the most subtle of linguistic points.

For those few among us who were enthusiastic about the study of grammar, Baron Ginzburg's course in that subject was no less than delightful.

We began with the *Zahot* of Ibn Ezra and went on to *Sefer ha-Reqma* of Yona Ibn-Genah for whom the Baron felt particular affection.

All these lessons and lectures were in essence merely a sort of entry hall to the great main chamber which was Maimonides' *Guide to the Perplexed*. The Baron never ceased to regret that because we made so little progress in our study of Arabic he could not teach us the *Guide* in the original. For him Maimonides was the central and ideal figure in Jewish intellectual history. There was symbolic evidence of this in the Baron's library. That huge collection, housed in many rooms and halls, opened onto a dark, small, intimate sort of room which was his private study—and a private doorway, one might say, to the sanctuary of Jewish and world thought. At the heart of his study, above a desk laden with the books, pamphlets, manuscripts, and proof sheets with which he was preoccupied, hung the only picture in the room. It was a medium-sized photograph of a portrait of Maimonides in a gilt frame.

During recesses or after class we argued heatedly with each other about general and Jewish problems, and the Baron listened intently, like a patient father who understood our youthful zeal. It was not unusual for him to invite one or another of us to come to see him and discuss ideas of ours which seemed mistaken to him. I remember how impressed I was by the delicacy with which he spoke to us on those occasions and the care he took not to attack concepts cherished by our generation, ideas which he was, in fact, most eager to dislodge from our minds.

I cannot forget the conversation in which he tried to open my eyes to the inadequacy—as he saw it—of the terms "nationalism" and "assimilation" which I used so frequently in discussions with my fellow students. When he felt that I remained unconvinced he resorted to an argument that seemed to him beyond dispute—the case of Maimonides. Could I possibly fit Maimonides into either of my two favorite categories? Was he a nationalist in his thinking? How could he have been, when he lived surrounded by the best in the world thought of his age, absorbed the wisdom of Greece, possessed all the intellectual treasures of the Arabs and wrote his books in Arabic, was friendly with non-Jewish rulers and groups, fought against the anthropomorphisms which generation after generation of our people had accepted as holy, and suffered persecution at the hands of the unyielding guardians of the past among us? On the other hand, could you call him an assimilationist? How could you, when he, more than any other Jew, elevated and sanctified Jewish thought according to all the concepts of science and philosophy? Was it not he who had fixed and consolidated the *halakhah* for his generation and those to follow, and who had formulated the precepts of the Creed that had become basic for all Judaism?

If my definitions were inapplicable to the great and primary figure, how could they be used to classify smaller men and events? Was it not, therefore, clear that the terms "nationalist" and "assimilationist," cherished by me and my contemporaries, failed to meet all the requirements of our complex situation and should be replaced or supplemented by other definitions?

I can still see him as he stood opposite me during that long talk. He, the teacher, leaned against the door post between his study and his library, and I, the student, tried to defend myself against his attack. I remember how agitated he was in spirit, how restrained and noble in argument—while above his head hung the picture of Maimonides. . . .

One of the disciplines which we students felt to be lacking and necessary was historical study of the social and economic life of Jews in the lands of the Diaspora. It was not easy to find a specialist in this field, and when Dubnow, whom we had impressed with our desire for such study, came at last to tell us that there was a fine young scholar available, Dr. M. L. Wischnitzer of Vienna, he added with restrained sadness that he feared the Baron would not agree to open the doors of the Academy to a course stressing the "new-fangled" social and economic approach.

We decided to try to appeal to Baron Ginzburg directly. We knew the warmth of his feelings for his Academy and its student body, and trusted that somehow we would succeed in gaining his consent.

He agreed to receive a delegation. There were three of us, and to this day I remember with absolute clarity the talk between us and the fatherly Baron. I had been charged with opening our case. There in the Baron's study, facing the picture of Maimonides, I spoke of the need for this new discipline and of the young scholar who was available. Excitedly, the Baron rose from his chair, leaned against the doorpost opening onto his great library, crossed one leg over the other, and said (as always in Russian, the language of the Academy's lectures): "Dear ones, I am deeply grieved by this request of yours. I am certain that you have no intention in the world of causing me unhappiness, and it is very difficult for me to say no to you. But how can I hide my concern from you? You have come here to study the nature and destiny of the Jewish people—and now I hear you asking to be taught what occupations Jews were compelled to engage in to keep alive. It is as if a scholar had been asked to lecture to you on Kant, and then, instead of teaching you the *Critique of Pure Reason*, spent his time describing the restaurant

Kant frequented and the kind of cutlets his wife gave him. And it is not Kant you are studying, but that sublime people God chose for His own! Do you really think it is so important to know exactly when the gentiles permitted us to engage in trade and when those malicious people forced us to be money-lenders? What good will the information do you? And wouldn't it be a pity to spend your precious time on this when there are still so many rooms in the mansion of Jewish scholarship that are closed to you and so many great books waiting for you?"

As he spoke, he pointed to the tens of rooms filled with bookshelves from floor to ceiling, endless, infinite treasure of books. . . .

We shrank before the majesty of his suppressed rage. And he, walking excitedly across the room between the desk and the books, suddenly stood still and went on even more bitingly: "If you do research on horses—there is such a science, too—it is obviously very important to investigate what fodder should be put in the horses' crib: oats or barley. But when the subject of your study is the wisdom of the chosen people, do you think that their fodder and their crib should concern you?"

And then, to point up further the vast distance between what seemed to him the correct approach to Jewish history and the one we had been misled into advocating, he said: "Do you know, dear ones, how I would lecture to you about the history of our people, if I were given the subject to teach? Suppose, for example, that we were dealing with the end of the Spanish Period. I would give a lecture of one hour on the enviable position occupied by the Jewish community in that country, the great contributions they made to its culture and political life, one of them even becoming Minister of the State, Don Isaac Abrabanel by name, born in year so and so, died in year so and so, and author of such and such books. This would be my material for one hour. The rest of the year would be spent on the contents of Don Isaac's books! *That* is true Jewish history, and that and only that is worthy of real study."

We saw that we had grieved the Baron greatly. We did not dare to appeal to him any further and we walked out unhappy, a little ashamed, and with no promise at all from him. But a week later, going into the lecture hall, we found a notice on the wall signed by the administration of the Academy. It announced the date on which Dr. M. L. Wischnitzer would begin to lecture on "The Economic History of the Jews"; students wishing to take the course were requested to register.

So, too, though he did not identify himself completely with the Zionist enthusiasm of many of us, the Baron—for our sakes—arranged visits to the Academy by a number of distinguished Zionists. I remember the coming of Dr. Ben-Zion Mossinsohn of the Herzlia Gymnasium, and Mordecai Ben-Hillel Ha-Cohen, and above all the utterly festive occasion of Chaim Nachman Bialik's visit. That day all the normal order of things was completely disarranged. And the next day when Bialik ate with us and asked me, I remember, whether a future great historian of the Jewish people, a future Zunz, was sitting at the table with us—our excitement and admiration knew no bounds.

Life was to scatter us far and wide in the lands of the Diaspora and in Israel. The Academy itself was closed during the Revolution and though attempts were made to reopen it, none of them proved successful. As for our teachers, some lived to a ripe old age and others died before their time. In the year when his seventieth birthday was to be celebrated, Buki Ben Yagli died; it was at the beginning of World War I and he was spared the dreadful things to come. Shimon Dubnow died a martyr's death with all the Jews of Riga when the Nazis destroyed the ghetto. Markon and Slossberg died in foreign lands, the former in Hamburg, the latter in Paris, both of them uprooted from the place of their work and influence, and doomed to be twice exiled. Only Dr. Wischnitzer and Rabbi Karlin were laid to eternal rest in the soil of *Eretz Yisrael.* Rabbi Karlin had been able to re-establish his household in Israel and to publish a number of his legal studies there; it was even given to him to participate in drafting the laws of the Jewish State. As for Dr. Wischnitzer, who had joined the faculty of Yeshiva University in New York, he spent the last months of his life in Israel, working out plans for a comprehensive study of the history of Russian Jewry and renewing his ties with relatives, friends and students who lived in Israel.

Only one of our teachers died while the Academy was still open and functioning: this was Baron Ginzburg himself. I was not in St. Petersburg during the vacation period of late summer 1910, when he was struck down by disease and forced out of active life. Returning after the Holy Days, I found that he was mortally ill and could be visited for no longer than a few moments.

Only a short time was to pass before we, his pupils, stood as mourners around his bed in his study. Spontaneously—no decision had been taken nor suggestion made—we began to recite the Psalms in the age-old fashion. We went on for long hours.

Though he died prematurely and the Academy was destroyed, he and all its staff live in our grateful recollection.

Grandfather's
Parting Gift

While I was growing up, I had no sterner critic than my devout grandfather, the fervent Habad *Hasid* who, though he lived in a town several miles away from ours, kept a keen and disapproving eye on me and my search for new ways of life. Though he learned to forgive his granddaughters much, he could not pardon my Zionist enthusiasm and my odd companions, and he never ceased trying to bring me back "to the right path." Yet there was no one dearer to me than this grandfather. From my early childhood, whenever I looked at him sitting at the head of the table, I sensed with wonder a sort of spiritual radiance shining from his high forehead. His learning had become part of me, his chants echoed throughout our house, and his ardor was to sustain me for many long years in all the wandering and searching of my life.

As long as I still lived at home and a good waggoner could bring us to Grandfather in two hours' time, frequent meetings sharpened the disagreements between us and at the same time strengthened the bond of affection. Grandfather visited us on the way to and from his rebbe before Shevuot and Rosh Hashanah; he spent some time in our summer cottage in the woods, and came to us for every important family event. On our part, we visited him during the weeks of Passover and Succot, on the anniversary of Grandmother's death and on the nineteenth of Kislev, memorial day of Habad. And every one of these encounters served to re-enforce the enduring love and the growing antagonism between us.

When I left the family for new and distant places of study, Grandfather began to seem far-removed, almost a vague memory. I was no longer terrified of his fanatical zeal, nor warmed by his inner light; and I no longer knew whether he was interested in my studies and activities. From my mother, his daughter, I learned that the death of his rebbe had left him terribly depressed and that he was growing more and more eager to leave Russia for Hebron, the Habad center in the Holy Land where his brother, too, had gone in old age. In fact, plans for his journey were being discussed by Mother and her brothers in the letters that passed between them.

In the summer of 1911, I was at last able to go to Palestine. I went home first and spent the last Sabbath before sailing with Grandfather. This was to be the last time Grandfather had a member of his family with him for Sabbath. Half a year later I received the news of his death.

During our day together I realized—to my shock and distress—how lonely his life was. To be sure, he lived within the boundaries of his own town, the town where he was born and spent all his years. But the town itself seemed somehow to have slipped out of its boundaries, while he remained there like the remnant of a dying legend, the last of a generation of giants, "a tamarisk in the desert," as the prophet said.

The town was Mir, old, distinguished, rich in tradition, noted for its yeshiva, long a fortress of Lithuanian scholarship. It was virtually another Volozhin, a sister to Aisheshok. Even in its most thriving years its economic opportunities were far from abundant, but its place as a center of learning was constant—in days of decline, as well as in earlier periods. I found the yeshiva still humming day and night with the voices of students. They came to it from great distances, even from the far-off, new Diaspora communities and among them were prodigies of intellect and of endless devotion to learning. Aside from the yeshiva, the town was growing more and more desolate. After each new fire—and fires were always breaking out—the youth of even the old and established families left for the larger, new cities of the region; their elders, remaining behind, seemed to become suddenly very aged. Among our own relatives all the young and prosperous were no longer to be found in the town. The long line of empty lots near the yeshiva was visible proof of the change.

The old, familiar figures whom I remembered from my childhood visits had died off one by one. Grandfather's older brother, for example, who had become wealthy in Hommel, was related by marriage to the Admor of Ladi, and was said to be so pious that on Sabbaths he covered his beard with a silk sack lest a single hair fall to the ground—he had long since sent his large library to Hebron and departed this life. There had been a younger brother whose business activity brought him frequently to Koenigsberg and who was thus considered the "German" in the family. Actually, even on the High Holy Days he took the liberty of praying not in a silk *kaftan* but in a dark fabric coat, while on Sabbaths he wore a high hat; in addition he used to say *Ja* rather than the Yiddish *Yeh.* He, too, was no longer among the living. Nor was Grandfather's nephew, who was the same age as Grandfather and as ardent a Habad *Hasid* as he. I remember how, despite a hoarse voice and extreme deafness, he used to sing the hymn of the angels, "*Bnei Heichala*," with infinite enthusiasm.

Of them all, Grandfather alone remained, like a solitary cliff on the shore of a lake that has dried up. The entire environment from which he sprang, in which he grew up, and with which he differed, seemed to be disappearing. Ever since the head of the yeshiva had taken as son-in-law the son of a founder of the *mussar* movement, and study of his Slabodka *mussar* penetrated into the old yeshiva, the breach between the yeshiva and the little group of *Hasidim* in Mir had grown even wider—and Grandfather even lonelier.

The hasidic group itself had shrunken and changed unrecognizably. Where was Reb Baruch Hashes, the lean, tall *Baal Tefilla*, who on Rosh Hashanah and Yom Kippur would chant the prayers for nearby villagers, his lion's voice thundering through the woods? And where was the old, blind *dayan* from Neswich, who was a fervent *Hasid* and at the same time an extraordinary example of Lithuanian scholarship, famous for his arbitration of complicated commercial disputes? Where had Yoshe the winemaker vanished to, he who was the brother of my teacher, Yaakov Meir? I had once seen Yoshe,

Slonimer *Hasid* that he was, climbing into my
grandfather's *succah* through a window; when I
asked him in surprise why he did not go through the
open door, he answered mockingly: "Am I a *Mitnaged* to go through a door?" And Velvel the *shamash*, chanter of the morning prayers in the *shtiebel*,
he who used to break my heart every time I heard
his deep, sad half-sigh, half-prayer on Mondays and
Thursdays: "Our brothers of the House of Israel, in
sorrow and captivity, whether on land or on sea. . . ."
Where was he? Where were they all? Gone in so few
years?

Towards evening on the Friday of my brief, last
visit I went with Grandfather to the synagogue to
welcome the Sabbath. Then I learnt that his *shtiebel*,
too, had perished. It had been destroyed during the
last fire and now all the remaining Habad *Hasidim*
assembled in a *minyan* that met for the time being
in the unfinished house belonging to one of the faithful members, a carpenter by trade. In this house that
was not yet a house, so workaday in atmosphere, its
scaffolding still not removed, bundles of wood scattered everywhere, the worshippers themselves seeming like accidental survivors of some catastrophe, in
this casual, unimpressive setting, Grandfather tow-
ered over his surroundings, awesome in his dignity
and his rare obstinacy of spirit.

Till my last moment I will remember Grandfather standing before the *minyan*, chanting the

prayers that welcome the Sabbath. He was thin and tall, and the narrow girdle on his black silk *kaftan* seemed to lend even further length to this figure that was all aspiration to the heavens. He looked as if he were standing on tiptoe; all his movements were directed upwards; even his pointed beard seemed raised. A candle burning in holiness on the eve of Yom Kippur—that was the image he brought to mind.

His prayer was a raging fire, kept in check and subdued. It rose from the depths within him to the source of consolation. My eager eyes, with those of all the assembly, were lifted to him. And it was during those flaming moments of prayer that Grandfather and I, his young antagonist, were reconciled. The power of his prayer and my spiritual participation in it bridged the differences between us—there was no discussion nor argument, "no speech nor language," as the Psalmist says.

Actually there had been a perverse occurrence which might have made our reconcilation almost impossible. My Party comrades in the town had learnt of my visit and my forthcoming *aliya,* and arranged a public meeting in my honor. My name leaped out of the advertisements they had posted. The meeting could not be kept secret from Grandfather and his friends, and I was full of fear that, as a result, my visit would only make the chasm between us wider. But when we prayed together, the fear was dissipated and the chasm disappeared. Listening to Grandfather chant, I heard beneath the words his deep lament over the cruel loneliness of his old age and the inexorable decline of the precious world that had been his. I heard his grief over the differences dividing kinsmen and at the same time his proud devotion to the immutable glory. I heard his passionate gratitude for the great bliss he felt in nearness to the source of all blessing; in the eternity of Israel unimpaired from generation to generation; and in the bond—at last—between my soul and his.

I can still hear Grandfather's voice chanting to his Father in Heaven, in the presence of his grandson on earth:

"Sanctuary of the King, city of sovereignty, rise, go forth from thy ruins. Too long hast thou sat in the vale of tears.

"He will lavish His pity upon thee . . . Cease to be ashamed and confused.

"Why art thou cast down and disquieted?

"The afflicted of my people trust in thee—the city shall be built upon its mound."

And then with complete resignation and understanding, Grandfather sang out the Sabbath Psalm in a hearty, rhythmic tune, a mood of purest thanksgiving:

"For Thou, Lord, hast made me glad through Thy work:

"I will exult in the works of Thy hands.

"How great are Thy works, O Lord! Thy thoughts are very deep.

"A brutish man knoweth not; neither doth a fool understand this. . . ."

That his Sabbath prayer was a gift to last all my years, Grandfather could hardly have known. And in the very last moments before my carriage moved, he gave me still another, utterly precious gift.

Except for set meetings with my comrades, I had spent the whole of the Sabbath and the hours of its departure on Saturday night in Grandfather's company. To the best of my recollection, we spoke very little about the family and not at all about controversial matters. It was scholarly discussion of Torah that occupied almost all the time, and both of us were overjoyed that I could still be somewhat of a match for him, though more as a listener than a talker. Whether he spoke of the mysteries of Hasidism or the rationality of Talmud, with his fellow-worshippers in the *shtiebel* or with the yeshiva students who came to visit him, or even when he sang his prayer melodies before his Creator—it seemed very clear to me that in a sense he was addressing me particularly, in the hope that his words, with all their connotations and all their special flavor, would enter my heart. And my heart was indeed wide open to receive them.

Early Sunday morning when the waggoner came

to take my valise, Grandfather put on his summer coat, opened his sunshade, and walked out with me to the end of town.

As he walked, sometimes pausing and standing still, he said something like this:

"My child, you know the melody of the Old Rav very well. There is something special about it that you should be told, something I learned from the old *Hasidim* in the rebbe's house.

"There are times when a man wants to remember a tune familiar to him and he simply cannot recall it no matter how hard he tries. On the other hand, there are times when a tune keeps humming in a man's mind and he does not want it or enjoy it but cannot get rid of it. In both cases it is clear that the tune—however good it may be—does not grow from the same root as the man's soul. He and the tune are two completely separate entities.

"But if a man can recall a tune whenever he wants to and it gives him pleasure each time, that is a sign that the tune is really his, deriving from the same source as the man's own soul.

"Thus, my child, the melody of the Old Rav is rooted in the soul of every Habad *Hasid* and his children and children's children until the end of the generations. If a righteous *Hasid* or any one of his descendants wants to remember this holy melody and it escapes him no matter how hard he tries to recall it, this simply proves that at that particular time he has deviated somehow from the true path and must search his soul and repent.

"It cannot be for nothing, my child, that a *Hasid* forgets the Rav's melody—this precious gift and touchstone. Do not lose it, my child!"

Our sages have said that men should part from each other while talking of the Law. Grandfather did just that. When he saw the waggoner hurrying me, he suddenly posed a complicated problem about sacrificial offerings of fruit of the Land and solved it by reference to a passage in Maimonides which he had just noted that week. Then he kissed me on the mouth and the wagon started to move.

Many stormy days have passed since then, but I have never forgotten how Grandfather stood under his sunshade in the middle of the road in the noon heat of a July day, at peace with his grandson and erstwhile antagonist, his lips murmuring the traditional blessing of parting, his moist, shining eyes fixed on the wagon as it moved away towards the Land he and all his people longed for, the Land that was at once his and his grandson's. His radiance will remain in my heart till its last beat, and his wonderful gift, too, is with me till this day.

In all the perplexities of my life whenever I have suddenly wished to remember the melody of the Old Rav and the good tune has responded, I have felt new strength welling up within me each time, evidence that my direction is right. All despair conquered, I have gone on my way in hope and inner peace.

Her Undimmed Light

It was the end of August, 1911 and I had been in the Land about three weeks. Behind me were a day in Jaffa, a Sabbath in Rishon le-Zion, a journey through the Judean villages, Tisha b'Av at the Wailing Wall, and a few days with the editors of the first Hebrew socialist paper, *Ahdut*, in Jerusalem. After all this, accompanied by Yitzhak Ahduti, I set out for Galilee. Yitzhak went as far as Merhavia where he was soon to meet a tragic death, and I, who was shortly to work at Merhavia, went north alone, so

that before starting to work I might meet with Berel
Katznelson at Kinneret.

For me, fresh from the northern climate of St.
Petersburg, the August heat was almost unbearable.
My friends advised me to travel by night and in the
very early morning, and I was most grateful to them
for this wise counsel. In the stillness of the night all
the mysterious loveliness of the country was revealed to me, and in the chill of dawn every step I
took on the desolate paths inscribed still another
letter in the covenant of life that was being sealed
between the Land of the Fathers and young son
returning from far away, after the shattering experience of Revolution and its aftermath. Torn by con-
flicts and thirsting for faith, this younger self of
mine was eager to undertake the good deed, prepared for the miracle.

Will I ever forget my climbing Mount Tabor at
night? The night before that I had accompanied
Joseph Nachmani in his watchman's rounds along
the stockade at the village of Yema, the Yavniel of
today: over and over again we scrutinized every in-
sect in the courtyard, every hole in the fence, and
for that one night, even though it was as a novice,
an amateur, a kind of tourist, I was, in a way,
Nachmani's partner, sharer in his work of self-defense. I slept all day after that and at night climbed
Tabor. Climbed? Actually I crawled on all fours.
With all my youthful energy I wrestled with that

mountain—until I conquered it. That calm, innocent, rounded height proved completely deceptive; neither calm nor innocent but one mass of cliffs and crevices, hills and valleys, hill facing hill, hill upon hill, narrow winding trails that climbed up and went down and vanished from sight in the pale moonlight. To reach the top became a matter of supreme importance to me; you might have thought it was the reason for my coming to the Land and that up there on the summit I expected to find salvation. I did not stop struggling until the dawn came and found me on the top of Mount Tabor; I was bitterly disappointed, to be sure, that I encountered no one but a Russian priest with a huge crucifix on his chest. . . .

The next day I heard that there was a much easier, well-trodden path which could have saved me all that trouble, but I have never ceased to be thankful for the good fortune which kept me ignorant of the easy path and left me to conquer Tabor as I did, by the sweat of my brow. From that day to this, for me there is no mountain like Tabor.

From there I rode on donkey back to Migdal, and at two o'clock in the chilly night set out on foot for Kinneret. The watchman at Migdal gave me some tea and told me how to go: "Keep to the lake shore all the way."

At every stage of our life in the Land one particular place has been the meaningful center, the symbol. Place has succeeded place, but at that time for me it was Kinneret. The independent *kvutza* had just been set up there, after the strike against Berman, the PICA manager; Hannah Meisel's Girls Training Farm was there; my friend, Joseph Saltzman, had gone there—that veteran member of Poale Zion who was imprisoned in Siberia, escaped and reached Vilna, where he slept in my bed, and then left illegally for Palestine, with our whole group escorting him to the railroad. Above all, Kinneret was the place where Berel Katznelson lived. I had never met him, but I had heard much about him from friends close to both of us in his native Bobroisk, who had also told him about me. I knew about his political past as a member of the S.S.; about his Zionism of the present and his doctrine of the *kvutza*, about his critical attitudes and the debates he waged so skillfully with my closest friends. I knew how ill he had been with typhus before his *aliya*—the disease, they said, "had cleansed him of Exile and everything connected with it." His new way of living as farm worker in a collective—the way he followed and taught others—should be called, I thought, "the way of Kinneret." It was a way that stirred me deeply.

That journey alongside of Lake Kinneret, the Sea of Galilee, was an unforgettable one. I was fresh from Jewish studies and, among other things, I had delved into the history of the Second Temple and done some reading in New Testament criticism. The figures of the past filled my mind and the lovely shores of Kinneret were full of life and speech for me that night. The shadows by the wayside were familiar and articulate, shades of the past, laden with memories that shone like torches in the darkness.

Suddenly high on a hill above the lake the courtyard of Kinneret revealed itself. The dawn broke, and as I climbed the hill, the lake grew constantly wider, gleaming at me in all the purity of its tranquil blueness. I had not quite reached the fence that surrounded the village when the bar of the gate was removed from within and the lively, cackling din of the farmyard filled the air. I made out the wonderful sound of a whole choir of birds, directed at a distance by an imperious voice speaking clear, majestic Hebrew. I stood stock-still, and then the gate opened and out of the yard issued a flock of white ducks, gabbling and jostling and sprawling all over the hillside, while behind them in a white dress walked a slim shepherdess, blue-eyed, lithe as a gazelle and lovely as Lake Kinneret. She held a palm branch in her hand, and with that scepter and her young, warm voice and graceful body—softness and strength combined—she dominated the whole rushing mass. In lyrical Hebrew she led the ducks at dawn from the farmyard of Kinneret to pasture.

Breathless, I hid behind the fence till the whole dazzling caravan had passed by.

That girl was Rachel, the poetess.

The next day a group of us climbed the hills on the other side of Lake Kinneret and rowed back to the *kvutza* in the moonlight. It was my impression that Rachel was not in the least concerned with me but concentrated all her attention on Berel. In a sense this was rather pleasing, for it made us members of the same small circle, a circle inspired and held together by the influence of "the older brother" who was our teacher. But there were others who sought to attract Rachel's interest. One of them was a shipmate of mine, of whom I had grown very fond during the voyage; he, too, came from St. Petersburg where he was the managing editor of the Russian educational monthly issued by the "Society for the Dissemination of Enlightenment among Jews" (I heard years later that after the Revolution he became one of the editors of the large *Soviet Encyclopedia*). During our long talks on the deck he had told me repeatedly that if he found the Land to his liking, he would cut all his ties with Russia and settle there. Incidentally I had learned from him that he planned to visit a friend who came from this town, a very charming and gifted girl, he said. He had not heard from her for a number of years and would look for her till he found her. We parted at Jaffa port and only met again that day in Kinneret, where I discovered that the girl he spoke of was none other than Rachel.

Joseph Saltzman was with us, too—my old "Siberian" friend from Vilna. He had become completely "assimilated" in the Land, turning into a model *shomer* who galloped on his horse, wore a belt of ammunition, was strong and proud and sensitive, his natural fairness darkened by the sun. He was the captive of Rachel's charm, pursuing even her shadow. It was literally pursuit, for when at one point Rachel hid from sight among the bushes, the faithful Joseph, terrified lest she lose her way among the unfamiliar mountains, leaped onto his horse and, without a word, rode off to look for her among the rocks. He circled around in that wasteland for more than two hours while she was with us all the time. She seemed totally unaware of what Joseph was doing and I at that time was incapable of understanding the mischievous pleasure she derived from teasing an admiring friend.

Yet actually there was no room in Rachel's heart for any of these rivals; she had been completely captured by the magic of Galilee and the marvellous spirit of antiquity, the proud spirit of Israel's childhood that was still to be felt in the desolate mountains across the Lake. Eight years later, describing that excursion of ours in a Russian sketch which appeared in the Odessa paper, *Yevreiskaya Missl*, she wrote: "We walked over ground that still bears the imprint of our Father Abraham's footsteps. We heard the echo of the word of God to him in ancient days:

'I will make of you a great nation, and I will bless you and make your name great.'"

Those hills across the lake were scorched and steep, their sides flinty rock. Every growing thing had been destroyed by the everlasting sun. There was neither blossom nor flower, only eternal peaks and yellow clods, consumed by the blasting heat. Suddenly in the sand Berel found a round stone: it was hollow and shaped like an upper millstone. Berel stood and looked at it, rubbed it and examined it, and then carefully explained to us that this must once have been part of an ancient water pipeline composed of stone rings, each so shaped at the edge as to be able to enter the next and become firmly attached to it. Galilee was known to have used such pipes in antiquity, and indeed the signs of the shaped edge were still visible in the stone. Clearly, these hilly lands had once been irrigated and populated— and could be populated again.

As I stood there with Berel, I was astounded by the vast contrast between the heights and the valley —two worlds geographically so close to each other. On the hillsides above, the day blazed like a furnace over a tawny stretch of death, while below there was life in abundance, bird and tree and shadow and flower, and a golden brook flowing in the wadi and a light breeze blowing at its leisure. Only some ancient carob trees grew up above and some branches pushing their way through the stones. The carobs grew on a slant, not upward but downward as if they, too, were drawn to the living valley and wadi, and lowered their old heads to receive the gay blessing of the fresh world down below.

Suddenly Rachel climbed up and stretched out on the trunk of a carob up on the top of a hill. From there, golden in the sunlight, her white dress glistening, she raised her voice high in song toward us, the group down in the wadi. We heard every note as if she were nearby, and we heard not only her voice but a powerful echo responding: the whole landscape sang in ancient Sephardi Hebrew, which seemed to have been preserved here in its purity. It was as if our far-off ancestors, shepherds and maidens of Israel, who went out into these mountains on some day of joy or mourning, had hidden those beautifully authentic, precisely articulated Hebrew sounds in the crevices of the rocks to be preserved there till the day of deliverance came. And the day was now beginning to come. Rachel called from the summit and the sounds came flying to her out of their stony hiding places, pure as on the day they were concealed, joyful as in the childhood of our people.

I was intoxicated by the heady wine of that echo. I even tried to put the emotion and the experience into verse. And seventeen years later Rachel's poems (particularly "The Echo" and "Covenant of the Echo") gave witness that she, too, had never forgotten the marvel of these sounds—

Echo in the mountains, clear and strong,
Echo in the mountains, O how long
I will remember you . . .

and

He said to her: 'Your voice comes from the past,
The voice of shepherds on Judea's hills.'

Of such a living legend one says in Rachel's own words: "The hosts of time cannot subdue it." Not even the hosts of death.

War Against War

☆

The First Congress of the Socialist International which I was privileged to witness was in fact the last congress attended by representatives of all streams of thought and ideological systems within world socialism. From then on all socialist, communist and "third" congresses were meetings of only one of the lopped-off limbs of the movement (except for a Berlin conference of all three Internationals, which in effect proved that what divided them was much stronger than what united them).

"My" Congress was the last held by the un-

divided International. After it the rock crumbled—
that rock upon which, as Lasalle had put it, the
shrine of liberated mankind's future was to be built.
The time was December, 1912 and January, 1913.
The world was already scorched by the fire of war:
it had just died down in the Balkans and threatened
to break out again on all sides. The incendiaries
were at work; the seeds of conflict were being skillfully sown in various lands. Among the General Staffs
surveying their weapons and among the providers
of weapons in the offices of the armament factories,
impatience was growing. Signs of the approaching
conflagration—which was to start in August, 1914,
go on unchecked for four years, and consume mil-
lions of lives—were already obvious to perceptive
observers.

For the fathers of socialism and their faithful
followers, the movement's international aspect was
as basic and firmly held a concept as socialist doctrine itself. It was utterly inconceivable to them that
the two could be separated, whether in theory or
propaganda. Support for war between the nations
was as intolerable as propaganda against class
struggle. The movement, by force of its nature and
mission, had to organize a militant campaign against
both tendencies.

With the danger growing very near and the
hostile powers already assembling their forces, the
Socialist International summoned an extraordinary

world congress in Basel to consider plans for "waging war against war." That was the slogan above the entrance to the Münster where the Congress sat and that was the theme of its discussions and speeches. The delegates came from all affiliated countries, representing all varieties of opinion in the movement and including its most distinguished leaders and orators—old and venerated teachers of the doctrine as well as gifted young people at the beginning of their activity.

I was then a beginning student at the University of Freiburg in the province of Baden, two hours by rail from Basel, where the Congress was to be held. I had come to the University with a little money earned by writing on historical subjects for *The Russian-Jewish Encyclopedia* but three months in Freiburg had cut down my funds dangerously. There was still another difficulty: since our Poale Zion Party had as yet no connection with the International, I could not even get a card admitting me to the sessions. But I was determined to go, and at the last moment a fellow-student at the University put me in touch with a Warsaw daily which wired me an assignment as its correspondent at the Congress. My credentials were accepted and I was off.

The organizer of the Congress was Victor Adler, the leader of Austrian socialism, who prepared his movement to become a large, comprehensive and bold Party of the laboring class. With an eye to the

Party's future role he systematically trained leaders for key posts from among the young intellectuals who surrounded him, most of them to be sure of Jewish origin. His son Friedrich was one of them, as well as Friedrich's close friend, Otto Bauer, and the latter's opponent, Karl Renner. So was Ellenbogen, the press man and organizer of the Party; Helferding, the Marxist economist, whom Adler later advised to go to Germany; and Max Adler, the philosopher, who, encouraged by Victor Adler, found his way to teaching at the University of Vienna.

It was after years of guiding not only the Austrian but all the German-speaking socialist parties that the aging Adler undertook to lead the complicated and diversified Basel Congress which could succeed at all only if it was organized superbly well and which had an educational role to play within the movement that was no less significant than its propaganda role without.

A rich tradition of thought and action found expression in the speeches made by all the delegates. They themselves were the elect of the socialist movement. To me, youngster that I was, they seemed to represent the very highest in humanity.

There were two great, old socialist doctrinaires present, who shed the lustre of the First International and Marx himself upon the Congress and were venerated by all the delegates. These were Karl Kautsky and Eduard Bernstein, long-time ideo-

logical antagonists. Echoes of the great debate between them—between Orthodox Marxism and socialist Revisionism—had resounded throughout world
socialism since 1898 and was still carried on in the
organs of the Movement, the *Neue Zeit* of Kautsky
and the *Sozialistische Monatshefte* of Bernstein and
Bloch. Adler was overjoyed when he succeeded in
seating both of them on the dais together and having
them jointly express their wrath against the war-
mongers and jointly urge the workers of the world
"not to let the deadly crime be committed."

Kautsky looked older than Bernstein and his
voice was weaker. He was short, with a little beard
that had turned completely white. His wife Ilsa, always his assistant, never left his side. His analysis of
the movement in various countries showed complete
familiarity with the situation in each. As for Eduard
Bernstein, he had, I thought, the grave intellectual
face of a Lithuanian rabbi; his large beard was not
yet completely white. His calm, smiling manner of
speech was that of a wise man who understands his
opponents, of a historian who delights in making
comparisons and drawing contrasts. But when he
began to describe the tragedy war would bring and
the destruction of civilization that would come about
in its wake, his voice, suddenly youthful, thundered
with the vigor of a great moral preacher. Years later,
at the end of the War, when I met with him in Germany fairly often and he began to appear on our

Poale Zion platforms as a faithful supporter of our objectives and activities, I grew increasingly fond of him and I was deeply impressed by the authentic Jewishness of his personality.

As I remember it, the most powerful German orator at the Congress was August Babel. He was simple and direct, convincingly logical, refined and pleasant-mannered. All Russian socialists were brought up on translations of his brochures, and I myself only two years earlier had prepared the Yiddish version of his pamphlet on the General Strike. We Labor Zionists often appreciatively quoted his attack on anti-Semitism as the folly of the German "little man" for whom hatred of Jews served "as a substitute for socialism." The definition proved very useful in our debates with Bundists. At Basel I took pleasure in trying to grasp the complete significance of every word he said and the complete intention behind the significance of the words.

A German colleague of Babel's, the hot-tempered, keen old Wilhelm Liebknecht, was his peer in ability and influence, while the eldest member of the Swiss delegation, Hermann Greilich, was the perfect type of a rugged peasant. A square white beard covered his whole chest and his voice rang in our ears. He, too, was one of the surviving members of the First International and was listened to reverently at Basel. Among the representatives of the Czech Party were two with paradoxical names: a German named "Czech" and a Czech named "Nemetz," which means "German."

Russian socialism was represented in all its variants: There was Plekhanov whose writings on "The Monistic View of History" (under the pseudonym of Beltov) were our oracle. There was Alexinsky, who in the Duma spoke out so forcefully against the flunkies of the Czar, and Martov-Cederbaum who was then considered the spokesman of the movement's left wing. Of the socialist revolutionaries Rabinovitz came and the black-bearded young Victor Chernov, together with the aged Yegor Yegorovitz Lazarev whose folk-quality and shrewdness brought to mind some wandering sage among Gorki's characters. From Russian Poland came Dashinsky and Diamond of the Polish Socialist Party (PPS) and Rosa Luxemburg of the Polish Social Democratic Party (PSD). From Georgia, I remember, there was a whole delegation. Was there any one from the Bund? Perhaps Abramovitz from the Russian branch of the movement.

The Russians all seemed preoccupied with separate or joint conferences of their factions and rarely spoke in the general assembly. Russian was not yet one of the languages of the International. On the other hand, the renowned old English labor leader, Keir Hardie, made many speeches and graced all the important sessions. For both delegates and correspondents every one of his speeches was an event

—and a subject for lively discussion in the corridors. He was famed for his moral honesty and diplomatic skill, and at the Congress he simply tore to bits all the widely accepted assumptions that the masses craved war and conquests born of slaughter.

The second great orator in English, Morris Hillquit, reinforced and echoed Hardie. His manner of speech was that of a brilliant lawyer, and despite the differences in appearance and ideas, he reminded me forcibly of Vinaver, the St. Petersburg advocate.

Along with many other delegates I listened to the English—and not only the English—speeches in translation, but this was a translation so elegant and graceful, so convincing and so marvellously done, that we hardly regretted not understanding the original. The much-admired translator, Angelica Balabanova, was a fiery little woman, as much at home in many languages as in her native Russian. With the unflagging energy of youth and boundless verbal resources she turned Italian into French and French into English and all three of them into German. It was like watching a magician.

There were two other very well known women at the Congress, Lilli Braun and Klara Zetkin. Their protest against war, spoken in the name of the world's mothers, left all of us shaken.

But all that I heard from all the speakers at the Congress could not compare in impressiveness, uniqueness, exaltation—revelation, if you will—with the oration of Jean Jaurès, the like of which I had never known.

Though I did not understand his French at all—this time I did not wait for Balabanova's translation—I *felt* the meaning of his words. It was not only with his lips that he spoke, but with his hands and his feet, his elbows and his knees, with every movement of his body, rising and falling, trembling and darting—filling the whole of the platform with his presence. All his bones, as Scripture says, spoke. Spoke? They cried out, raged, threatened, warned, swore solemnly, fought the battle of the Lord. I knew then that it was the Prophet of Socialism that I was listening to.

And when Balabanova rose, moved and excited and full of excuses for daring to translate the vision of the seer into the language of ordinary mortals, and then transmitted Jaurès' thoughts in rich and picturesque German, I heard the actual text, the mystic undertones of which I had already grasped, and I understood what it was that had so overwhelmed me.

Jaurès had begun by speaking about the ancient church in which we were meeting and from which the ecclesiastical pictures and vessels had been taken out to be replaced by red flags. Christianity, he said, had held out a great promise to suffering humanity, but the violation of this promise by Christian aggressors and exploiters through the ages and left men bitterly disillusioned. The sacred ideals of redemption which had won the hearts of masses for the faith were now being trodden underfoot by alleged Christians. Thus it was that international socialism, which was fighting for peace among the nations, had the moral right to substitute its flags for the appurtenances of the religion whose promise had been broken; indeed the moral right brought a moral obligation with it. And Jaurès warned the world, described the horrors that would come with war, called upon faithful socialists to stand together like a fortified wall, warding off destruction and destroyers: "Let our lifeblood be our pledge! If the villains go to the slaughter, it will have to be over our bodies. . . ."

The flame in his words set the whole Congress on fire. Spontaneously the delegates all rose to their feet and took a solemn vow. It was proposed that socialists obligate themselves not to vote for military budgets. The motion was carried. It was proposed that a general strike be proclaimed throughout the world, if war broke out. The motion was carried.

The mighty sound of the *Internationale* being sung by the whole assembly filled the lofty, old Münster. . . .

Moshe Beilinson who, like me, was studying in the university town of Freiburg, had come with me to the Congress. He was about to complete his medical studies, while I had just begun history. Our acquaintance was only a few months old, and the joint journey to Basel was perhaps our first joint undertaking. He, too, listened to Jaurès and was full of praise for his message. Yet I noted that Beilinson's fine face was clouded by profound melancholy, the reason for which was not clear to me.

On the train taking us back to Freiburg, he said something like this: "Do you trust them? Don't for a moment! They will never keep that vow they took. The instant war is declared all of them will go crawling to the slaughter. Today there is no one—absolutely no one—whose word can be taken as truth. The wretched human race cannot rely on any force to check this madness. We are abandoned to fate. If we want to create a force for truth, we will have to begin everything from the beginning again."

Then he started to tell me what he was later to finish in my attic room—how enamored he had once been of the Russian revolutionary leaders; how completely he had believed in them and in their determination to translate their vision into reality; and what a dreadful blow it had been for him to learn that the actual life of the Party was altogether out of accord with the ideals of its vision.

The thrusting pain of his disillusionment was unbearable. It was quite clear that if he should choose "to begin everything from the beginning again" among us in the Land, the benefit to our work would be inestimable.

Before twenty months had passed the vow taken

so solemnly by the delegates in Basel was broken by almost all of them. They had forgotten.

But Jean Jaurès neither forgot nor went back on his word. The world around him, thirsting for blood, knew very well that this was a man who would not change; the bloody sacrifice could not begin unless his pure blood was shed the day before. . . .

And Beilinson, too, did not forget. He joined us in Palestine and "began everything from the beginning again."